Using the
**Common Core
State Standards** for

English
Language Arts

With Gifted and
Advanced Learners

Using the **Common Core State Standards** for English Language Arts With Gifted and Advanced Learners

Edited by
Joyce VanTassel-Baska, Ed.D.

Contributing Authors
Joyce VanTassel–Baska, Ed.D. • Claire E. Hughes, Ph.D.
Jennifer L. Jolly, Ph.D. • Todd Kettler, Ph.D.
Debra A. Troxclair, Ph.D. • Susan K. Johnsen, Ph.D.

A Service Publication of the

PRUFROCK PRESS INC.
WACO, TEXAS

Library of Congress Cataloging-in-Publication Data

Using the common core state standards for English language arts with gifted and
advanced learners / edited by Joyce VanTassel-Baska ; contributing authors, Joyce
VanTassel-Baska ... [et al.]
    p. cm.
Includes bibliographical references.
ISBN 978-1-59363-992-1 (pbk.)
1. Language arts--Standards--United States. 2. Gifted children--Education--United
States. I. VanTassel-Baska, Joyce.
LB1576.U77 2013
372.6--dc23
                    2012027518

Edited by Jennifer Robins

Production design by Raquel Trevino

ISBN-13: 978-1-59363-992-1

At the time of this book's publication, all facts and figures cited are the most current available. All telephone numbers, addresses, and website URLs are accurate and active. All publications, organizations, websites, and other resources exist as described in the book, and
all have been verified. The editor and Prufrock Press Inc. make no warranty or guarantee
concerning the information and materials given out by organizations or content found at
websites, and we are not responsible for any changes that occur after this book's publication.
If you find an error, please contact Prufrock Press Inc.

Prufrock Press Inc.
P.O. Box 8813
Waco, TX 76714-8813
Phone: (800) 998-2208
Fax: (800) 240-0333
http://www.prufrock.com

Table of Contents

Foreword

In the fall of 2011, at the annual retreat of the Board of Directors of the National Association for Gifted Children, an urgent request for guidance about the Common Core State Standards (CCSS) and their relationship to gifted programming and curriculum was heard from every corner of the membership. NAGC leaders and experts responded, starting with a meeting of the NAGC Association Editor, co-chairs of the Professional Standards Committee, the chair of the Education Committee, and the NAGC President and Executive Director at the 2011 annual convention in New Orleans. An ambitious plan was developed to address the needs of gifted education specialists and teachers regarding how to integrate the CCSS with their current programming and curricula.

Out of that meeting came the idea to develop two booklets, one on the English language arts standards and one on the mathematics standards. All involved shared a heartfelt sense of urgency about the importance of this task. The Professional Standards Committee went to work immediately, spending evenings at the conference crafting initial informational materials on the CCSS to distribute via the NAGC website.

The Common Core State Standards are a significant milestone affecting education in the United States. As of this printing, 45 states have adopted the CCSS, attesting to the collective concern about the quality of education in our nation and the commitment to improve it. The CCSS embody significantly higher expectations for learning and thus, if implemented with fidelity, have the potential to dramatically alter achievement for all students.

Gifted educators are excited about the CCSS, as they reflect many of the strategies that the field of gifted education has been stressing for decades as important to deep learning and engagement and high achievement—high-level, analytical thinking and advanced problem-solving skills. However, the CCSS alone will not ensure that gifted children receive the advanced content, accelerative options, and high-level enrichment that they need to be challenged and make continuous progress in their areas of talent. Hence the need for these booklets: They will help educators understand how to use the CCSS as a foundation and go beyond them for those learners who meet the standards earlier and faster. The booklets also assist educators in coupling and integrating the CCSS with gifted education curricula, instructional practices, and program models. These booklets are a valuable resource for all educators, not just those who work specifically in gifted programs. The reality is that most gifted children receive their instruction from teachers in heterogeneous classrooms, and these booklets can help all educators differentiate content and instruction for high-ability learners.

I want to thank the members of the Professional Standards Committee and others, who worked diligently to respond so quickly to the needs expressed by NAGC members and to fast track the production of these booklets through their efforts in New Orleans and at a work weekend in February 2012, particularly co-chairs Joyce VanTassel-Baska and Susan Johnsen, Cheryll Adams, Rima Binder, Alicia Cotabish, Reva Friedman-Nimz, Claire Hughes, Jennifer Jolly, Bill Keilty, Todd Kettler, Wayne Lord, Chrystyna Mursky, Julia Roberts, Elizabeth Shaunessy,

Linda Sheffield, and Debra Troxclair. I also want to thank the NAGC staff members who edited and assisted with the production aspects of this project, especially Jane Clarenbach.

Paula Olszewski-Kubilius
NAGC President
2011–2013

Preface

The importance of strong curriculum in content areas for advanced learners is a basic consideration in all gifted programs nationwide. In no areas is this more needed than in English language arts and mathematics, as they constitute the cornerstones of learning in our schools at all stages of development. They also constitute important talent domains for the development of future professionals whose work is centered on the application of these subject areas.

Gifted education, through the National Association for Gifted Children (NAGC), has developed a set of curriculum, assessment, and learning environment standards for pre-K–grade 12 programs that promote careful curriculum planning, differentiated instructional approaches, and authentic learning assessments, all aspects of the work associated with the new Common Core State Standards (CCSS). However, it was clear to the Professional Standards Committee within the organization that the Gifted Programming Standards needed to be aligned to the new Common Core State Standards to ensure that the CCSS are appropriately adapted and differentiated for our best learners.

The group has worked over the past several months to draft two guides (one in English language arts and one in mathematics) for practitioners that provide such translations for use in an array of settings that contain advanced learners—from cluster-grouped classrooms to pull-out programs to special classes to special schools. The guides provide examples of the relevant CCSS, matched to a suggested activity for typical learners and then differentiated for advanced learners. Assessment examples are also provided, including appropriate rubrics. Related material on further alignment to 21st century skills, to collaboration for interdisciplinary adaptations, and to professional development are included for easy referencing.

We sincerely hope these booklets will be used to ensure that advanced learners experience a rich and challenging curriculum as a result of the new CCSS and that practitioners use the examples as a model for their own continued curriculum work on behalf of advanced learners.

Joyce VanTassel-Baska, Ed.D., and Susan K. Johnsen, Ph.D.
Co-Chairs
Professional Standards Committee
National Association for Gifted Children

Acknowledgments

From concept to publication, there are a number of experts in English language arts, curriculum, pedagogy, and standards who volunteered their time and energy to support the development of this book. We value all of the contributions, but we would be remiss if we did not mention key participants from different stages of the book's creation.

First, we acknowledge the leadership of NAGC president Paula Olszewski-Kubilius, who, in response to emerging calls for assistance from NAGC members, made this book a priority for the organization. We naturally turned to our colleagues on the NAGC Professional Standards Committee and other experts involved in gifted education standards for assistance. These volunteers helped develop the Common Core State Standards materials at the 2011 NAGC convention in New Orleans that provided an initial framework for these books.

Recognizing that publications are strengthened through a rigorous review process, we also want to thank the reviewers who took time to provide valuable advice and feedback for this volume: Kimberley Chandler, Catherine Little, Elizabeth Shaunessey, and Tamra Stambaugh. We also appreciate the comments on the manuscript that we received from the Council of State Directors of Programs for the Gifted. All of the suggestions helped shape the final books.

Finally, there are others who have supported the development process, the content, and the need for the book. We thank Nancy Green and Jane Clarenbach at the NAGC national office, NAGC Association Editor Sidney Moon, and Joel McIntosh and Jennifer Robins at Prufrock Press.

Introduction

The purpose of this booklet is to provide classroom teachers and administrators examples and strategies to implement the new Common Core State Standards (CCSS) for English Language Arts for advanced learners at all stages of development in K–12 schools. One aspect of fulfilling that purpose is to clarify what advanced opportunities look like for such learners from primary through secondary grade levels. In other words, we want to demonstrate effective differentiation for top learners in English language arts (ELA). How can schools provide the level of rigor and relevance within the new standards as they translate them into experiences for gifted learners? How can they provide creative and innovative opportunities to learn what will nurture the thinking and problem solving of our best students in ELA?

This booklet also serves as a primer for basic policies and practices related to advanced learners in school. At all levels, schools must be flexible in the implementation of policies related to acceleration, waivers, and course credit, all of which may impact gifted learners. The developers of the CCSS acknowledged that advanced learners may move through the standards more readily than other learners (National Governors Association [NGA]

& Council of Chief State School Officers [CCSSO], 2010a), attesting to the importance of using differentiated approaches for these students to attain mastery and/or progress in academic achievement at their level. It is critical that schools allow for flexibility in these areas and others in order to accommodate our advanced learners.

In this booklet, we also want to demonstrate a trajectory for talent development in language arts that lends vision to the work of teachers as they deliver classroom instruction at one level but prepare students for the succeeding levels in the journey toward the real world of language-based careers. What is the progressive development of skills, habits of mind, and attitudes toward learning needed to reach high levels of competency and creative production in language-related fields? How does the pathway from novice to expert differ among promising learners? What is the trajectory for children of poverty with respect to time and effort, and how does it differ from that of more advantaged learners?

The booklet also includes multiple resources in the appendix material to support educators in developing and modifying materials for students who are advanced in English language arts. In addition to including a list of definitions of the key terms used in the booklet (Appendix A), we have included a research base of best practices in gifted education (Appendix B).

This booklet is also based on a set of underlying assumptions about the constructs of giftedness and talent development that underpin the thinking that spawned this work. These assumptions are:

- Giftedness is developed over time through the interaction of potential with nurturing environmental conditions. The process is developmental, dynamic, and malleable.
- Many learners show preferences for particular subject matter early and continue to select learning opportunities that match their predispositions if they are provided with opportunities to do so. For many children, especially those in poverty, schools are the primary source for relevant opportunities to develop domain-specific poten-

tial, although markers of talent development also emerge from work done outside of school in co-curricular or extracurricular contexts.

- Aptitudes may emerge as a result of exposure to high-level, challenging activities in an area of interest. Teachers should consider using advanced learning activities and techniques as a stimulus for all learners.

- In the talent development process, there is an interaction effect between affect and cognition, leading to heightened intrinsic motivation of the individual and focus on the enjoyable tasks associated with the talent area. This dynamic tension catalyzes movement to the next level of advanced work in the area.

- Intellectual, cultural, and learning diversity among learners may account for different rates of learning, different areas of aptitude, different cognitive styles, and different experiential backgrounds. Working with such diversity in the classroom requires teachers to differentiate and customize curriculum and instruction, always working to provide an optimal match between the learner and her readiness to encounter the next level of challenge.

Users of this booklet should note that the ideas contained herein are not intended to apply exclusively to identified gifted students; they also apply to those students who show an interest and readiness to learn within the domain of English language arts. Students with high potential and advanced readers would be candidates for a differentiated ELA curriculum.

Finally, it is our hope that this booklet provides a roadmap for meaningful national, state, and local educational reform that elevates learning in English language arts to higher levels of rigor for gifted—and, indeed, all—learners who can benefit from the elevation of task demands suggested.

The Common Core State Standards

The Common Core State Standards for English Language Arts are K–12 content standards that illustrate the curriculum emphases needed for students to develop the skills and concepts required for the 21st century. Adopted by 45 states to date, the CCSS are organized into key content domains and articulated across all years of schooling and, when adopted, replace the existing state content standards. The initiative has been state-based and coordinated by the National Governors Association (NGA) and the Council of Chief State School Officers (CCSSO). Designed by teachers, administrators, and content experts, the CCSS are intended to prepare K–12 students for college and the workplace.

The new CCSS are evidence-based, aligned with expectations for success in college and the workplace, and informed by the successes and failures of the current standards and international competition demands. The new standards stress rigor, depth, clarity, and coherence, drawing from the National Assessment of Educational Progress (NAEP) Frameworks in Reading and Writing (National Assessment Governing Board [NAGB], 2008, 2010). They provide a framework for curriculum development work, which remains to be done—although many states are already engaged in the process. States such as Indiana, Minnesota, Illinois, and Maine are working within and across local districts to design relevant curriculum and to align current practices to the new standards.

Rationale for the Work

The adoption of the Common Core State Standards in almost every state is cause for gifted education as a field to reflect on its role in supporting gifted and high-potential learners appropriately in the content areas. The field of gifted education has not always differentiated systematically in the core domains of learning, but rather has focused on interdisciplinary concepts, higher level skills, and problem solving, typically across domains. With the new CCSS and their national focus, it becomes critical to show how to differentiate for gifted learners within a set of standards that are reasonably rigorous in each subject area.

It has been stated by some that the standards do not require any special differentiation for the gifted—and may actually obviate the need for gifted education services because the standards are already at such a high level. Unfortunately, although the standards are strong, they are not sufficiently advanced to accommodate the needs of most gifted learners. Some students will traverse the standards before the end of high school (NGA & CCSSO, 2010a), which will require educators to provide advanced content for them. Beyond accelerative methods, however, there is also a need to enrich the standards by ensuring that there are open-ended opportunities to meet the standards through multiple pathways, more complex thinking applications, and real-world problem-solving contexts. This requires a deliberate strategy among gifted educators to ensure that the CCSS are translated in a way that allows for differentiated practices to be employed with gifted and high-potential students.

As with all standards, new assessments will likely drive the instructional process. Educators of the gifted must be aware of the need to differentiate assessments that align with the CCSS as well. Gifted learners will need to be assessed through performance-based and portfolio techniques that are based on higher level learning outcomes and that often vary from the more traditional assessments the CCSS may employ.

Although the CCSS appear to be a positive movement for all of education, it is important to be mindful of the ongoing need to differentiate appropriately for top learners. As a field, it is also critical to agree on the need to align with this work so gifted education's voices are at the table as the CCSS become one important basis, along with the newly revised InTASC Model Teacher Standards (CCSSO, 2011), for elevating teacher quality and student learning nationwide.

Alignment to 21st Century Skills

This booklet includes a major emphasis on key 21st century skills (Partnership for 21st Century Skills, n.d.) in overall orientation as well as in activities and assessments employed in the examples. Several of these skill sets overlap with the differentiation emphases discussed below in relation to the gifted standards.

The skills receiving major emphases in the booklet examples include:

- *Collaboration*: Students are encouraged to work in dyads and small groups of four to carry out many activities and projects, to discuss readings, and to plan presentations.
- *Communication*: Students are encouraged to develop communication skills in written, oral, visual, and technological modes.
- *Critical thinking*: Students are provided with models of critical thought that are incorporated into classroom activities, questions, and assignments.
- *Creative thinking*: Students are provided with models of creative thinking that develop skills that support innovative thinking and problem solving.

- *Problem solving*: Students are engaged in real–world problem solving and learn the processes involved in such work.
- *Technology literacy*: Students use technology in multiple forms and formats to create generative products.
- *Information media literacy*: Students use multimedia to express ideas and key learnings.
- *Cross-cultural skills:* Students read and discuss works and events representing the perspectives of different cultures and people.

Because these skills are relevant to all learners, the way they are addressed in the differentiated examples that follow is important for educators, as it shows the translation of the skills at higher levels and at earlier stages of development for gifted learners.

Differentiating the Common Core State Standards for Gifted and Advanced Students

Differentiation is based on an understanding of the characteristics of gifted and high-potential students *and* the content standards within a domain. The new Common Core State Standards provide an opportunity for the field of gifted education to examine its practices and align them more fully to the 2010 NAGC Pre-K–Grade 12 Gifted Programming Standards for curriculum, instruction, and assessment. Because the gifted programming standards for curriculum require us to engage in two major tasks in curriculum planning—alignment to standards in the content areas and the development of a scope and sequence—using the CCSS is a natural point of departure. The effort must occur in vertical planning teams within districts and states in order to ensure consistency and coherence in the process. There are four major strategies that may be employed to accomplish this task for gifted education:

- *Provide pathways to accelerate the CCSS for gifted learners.* Some of the CCSS address higher level skills and concepts that should receive focus throughout the years of schooling, such as a major emphasis on the skills of argument. However, there are also more discrete skills that may be clustered across grade levels and compressed around higher level skills and concepts for more efficient mastery by gifted students.

- *Provide examples of differentiated task demands to address specific standards.* Standards such as the research standard in English language arts lend themselves to differentiated interpretation through demonstrating what a typical learner on grade level might be able to do at a given stage of development versus what a gifted learner might be able to do. The differentiated examples should show greater complexity and creativity using a more advanced curriculum base in English language arts. Whereas typical learners might learn the parts of speech and practice their application across grades K–8, gifted learners might instead explore the relationship of these parts of speech and their function in different sentence patterns at an earlier stage of development. Other degrees of differentiation may take place by adding complexity to the tasks and using enrichment techniques that address student needs and district demographics.

- *Create interdisciplinary product demands to elevate learning for gifted students and to efficiently address multiple standards at once.* Because English language arts and mathematics standards can be grouped together in application, much of the project work that gifted educators might already use could be revised to connect to the CCSS and show how multiple standards could be addressed across content areas. For example, research projects could be designed to address the research standard in English language arts and the data representation standard in mathematics by (a) delineating a product demand for research on an issue, (b) asking researchable questions that require quantitative approaches, (c) using multiple sources to answer them, (d) collecting data, (e) interpreting data (e.g., by creating a scatterplot and deciding if there is a line of best fit and describing the related variables), and then (f) representing findings in tables, graphs, and other visual displays that are explained in text and presented to an audience with implications for a plan of action. Such a project might be possible for the gifted learner at an earlier grade than for a typical learner.

- *Create differentiated assessments to demonstrate gifted student authentic learning.* The use of alternative assessments to calibrate the extent to which gifted students are performing at appropriately advanced levels in the areas of language arts is also a critical consideration in differentiating the Common Core State Standards. The language arts curriculum should employ high-quality pre–post performance-based assessments to ensure that growth is being attained in higher level skills and concepts. The use of product assessment for long-term work coupled with pre–post writing and literary analysis assessments annually should be used to justify differentiated curriculum and instruction. Critical thinking and creative thinking growth should also be assessed.

General Approaches to Differentiating the English Language Arts Standards

The Common Core State Standards for English Language Arts identify K–12 grade-level literacy performance expectations in reading, writing, speaking, listening, and language, with specific benchmarks by grade for developmental progress. The ELA standards were designed to prepare students to become critical consumers of literature and informational texts across disciplines and are primarily framed as developmental processes that these students would be able to demonstrate by the end of a given grade level of instruction. As is noted in the ELA standards' preamble (NGA & CCSSO, 2010a), the curriculum, instruction, and scope of learning are not prescribed. Educators are given great latitude in how to obtain these achievement goals and in deciding which learning goals to infuse into the curriculum module.

Preassessment. Guided by assessment data, the ELA standards suggest that teachers are responsible for tailoring learning experiences for gifted students to foster the continued development of advanced skills, knowledge, and conceptual understanding. Instructional approaches in reading, for example, could include matching gifted readers with texts that are commensurate with or slightly above their documented reading level. Gifted and high-potential readers may also benefit from other instructional approaches recognized as beneficial for advanced readers, such as Socratic seminars.

Creative production. In line with the ELA standards' recommendations regarding continued development of student research skills, teachers of the gifted may also infuse opportunities for research in students' areas of interests as well as creative production. Teachers of gifted writers may encourage the development of advanced writing skills through writing competitions, production in public venues, or staging of a student's original writing through drama, poetry readings, mentorships with local writers or other writing experts, or in-class response groups comprised of classmates with similar advanced writing abilities.

Focus on concepts, issues, and themes. Teachers of gifted and high-potential students also should be mindful of the importance of providing conceptual units of study that foster interdisciplinary thinking, examination of complex issues, problem finding, and problem solving to stimulate discussion, debate, reasoning, and related skills of persuasion, which are progressively targeted as learners move from K–6 through secondary education.

Instructional pacing. Instructional pace is also a critical consideration in the education of gifted students. Curriculum should be made more advanced and challenging in an area or areas in which a student excels, based on the student's rate of learning. For example, a student who enters kindergarten reading at the second-grade level should receive instruction pitched at third-grade books and materials with matching comprehension questions and writing assignments. Teachers are responsible for monitoring the pace at which a gifted learner responds and adjusting pacing accordingly.

Specific Examples of Differentiating for Gifted and Advanced Students

The activities that follow are based on sample performance tasks and exemplars of reading text complexity, quality, and range that were developed by the writers of the Common Core State Standards for English Language Arts (NGA & CCSSO, 2010b). One column contains activities for typical learners, and the next column shares how activities can be differentiated for advanced learners.

Subject: ELA Reading Standards for Literature

The following examples, which represent appropriate-level activities for typical and advanced students, focus on several aspects of differentiation. The activities for advanced students are more abstract and idea-based than those designed for typical learners. They are more complex, requiring gifted learners to think at multiple levels simultaneously and work with more variables than the typical learner. By providing product choice, they also offer multiple creative opportunities for gifted learners.

Strand and Number: Key Ideas and Details #1

Grade-Level Outcomes in Knowledge and Skills: Read closely to determine what the text says explicitly and to make logical inferences from it; cite specific textual evidence when writing or speaking to support conclusions drawn from the text.

Grade and Standard	Typical Learners	Advanced Learners
Grade 3 RL.3.1. Ask and answer questions to demonstrate understanding of a text, referring explicitly to the text as the basis for the answers.	Students will ask and answer student- and teacher-created questions regarding the plot of Patricia MacLachlan's *Sarah, Plain and Tall*, explicitly referring to the text to form the basis of their answers.	Advanced students will ask and answer student- and teacher-created questions regarding what the plot of Patricia MacLachlan's *Sarah, Plain and Tall* says about courage and the life of women in the 19th century, using textual references. They will create a multimedia project that characterizes Sarah as a person of courage.

Grade and Standard	Typical Learners	Advanced Learners
Grade 5 RL.5.1. Quote accurately from a text when explaining what the text says explicitly and when drawing inferences from the text.	Students will select a line from Carl Sandburg's poem "Fog," and make an inference about what the author meant.	Advanced students will define personification, select a line from Carl Sandburg's poem "Fog," and describe how Sandburg uses personification to enhance his meaning. Students will create their own personification poem using "Fog" as a model or add an additional stanza to "Fog."
Grade 8 RL.8.1. Cite the textual evidence that most strongly supports an analysis of what the text says explicitly as well as inferences drawn from the text.	Students will identify one idea that is communicated in Carl Sandburg's poem "Chicago" and select lines of text to support their analysis. Students will write a poem about their own hometown using "Chicago" as a model.	Advanced students will describe how Sandburg's tone in "Chicago" changes from the beginning to the end of the poem, using textual evidence to support their analysis. Students will write a poem about their own hometown using "Chicago" as a model. Students can also create a multimedia presentation of the poem "Chicago" using music and color to illustrate tone in the poem.
Grades 11–12 RL.11–12.1. Cite strong and thorough textual evidence to support analysis of what the text says explicitly as well as inferences drawn from the text, including determining where the text leaves matters uncertain.	Students will cite strong and thorough textual evidence from John Keats's "Ode on a Grecian Urn" to support their analysis of what the poem says explicitly about the urn as well as what can be inferred about the urn from evidence in the poem. Based on their close reading, using a graphic organizer, students will draw inferences from the text regarding what meanings the figures decorating the urn convey and note where the poem leaves matters about the urn and its decoration uncertain.	At the end of "Ode on a Grecian Urn," Keats writes, "'Beauty is truth, truth beauty'—that is all Ye know on earth, and all ye need to know." Advanced students will develop a formal essay in which they explain what Keats meant, citing textual evidence from the poem to support their conclusion.

Subject: ELA Reading Standards for Informational Text

Like the examples provided to address the literature standard, the following examples focus on several aspects of differentiation. The activities for advanced learners are more abstract and idea-based than what would be expected for typical learners. They are more complex, requiring gifted learners to think at multiple levels simultaneously and work with more variables than the typical learner. By providing product choice, they also provide a creative context for advanced learners to express innovative ideas.

Strand and Number: Craft and Structure #6
Grade-Level Outcomes in Knowledge and Skills: Assess how point of view or purpose shapes the content and style of a text.

Grade and Standard	Typical Learners	Advanced Learners
Grade 3 RI.3.6. Distinguish their own point of view from that of the author of a text.	Students will read Kathleen V. Kudlinski's *Boy, Were We Wrong About Dinosaurs* and summarize the author's point of view about how the ancient Chinese were wrong about the dinosaurs.	Advanced students will read Kathleen V. Kudlinski's *Boy, Were We Wrong About Dinosaurs* and summarize the author's point of view about how the ancient Chinese were wrong about the dinosaurs and how this compares to present-day understandings. Using multimedia, students will create a presentation depicting the points of view of both the ancient Chinese and present-day people.

Grade and Standard	Typical Learners	Advanced Learners
Grade 5 RI.5.6. Analyze multiple accounts of the same event or topic, noting important similarities and differences in the point of view they represent.	Through selected readings, students will analyze multiple accounts of African American baseball players in the Negro leagues, noting similarities and differences of the various accounts.	Through selected readings, advanced students will analyze multiple accounts of African American baseball players in the Negro leagues, analyzing different perspectives towards racism and prejudice. Students will write a one-act play dramatizing multiple accounts of the players.
Grade 8 RI.8.6. Determine an author's point of view or purpose in a text and analyze how the author acknowledges and responds to conflicting evidence or viewpoints.	Students will review opinions from a Supreme Court case, determine each author's point of view, and summarize how he or she responds to the other viewpoints. Students will create a graphic organizer comparing the two points of view.	Advanced students will review opinions from a Supreme Court case, determine each author's point of view, summarize other viewpoints, and then prepare a written rebuttal to the author's point of view in the same format.
Grades 11–12 RI.11–12.6. Determine an author's point of view or purpose in a text in which the rhetoric is particularly effective, analyzing how style and content contribute to the power, persuasiveness, or beauty of the text.	Students will select a presidential inaugural address or State of the Union speech to determine the President's point of view and the elements of rhetoric used.	Advanced students will select two presidential speeches from two different periods and analyze the two President's points of view on issues and the use of rhetorical elements. Students will select one presidential speech and rewrite sections of the speech, switching from the rhetorical device used to others that represent current issues more dramatically.

Subject: ELA Standards for Writing

The examples provided to address the writing standard emphasize acceleration of content with respect to literary elements and the form of writing expected for advanced learners. They use multimedia at an earlier stage of development than the typical learner. The focus of the writing is also broader in scope, asking students to focus on global issues rather than local topics.

Strand and Number: Text Types and Purposes #1 (Opinion)

Grade-Level Outcomes in Knowledge and Skills: Write arguments to support claims in an analysis of substantive topics or texts using valid reasoning and relevant and sufficient evidence.

Note: This strand differentiation also contains differentiation of Standards 4–6: Production and Distribution of Writing.

Grade and Standard	Typical Learners	Advanced Learners
Grade 3 W.3.1. Write opinion pieces on topics or texts, supporting a point of view with reasons.	Students will write an opinion piece stating three reasons why their parents should give them a particular video game.	After selecting a local issue (e.g., building an amusement park near a historic battlefield), advanced students will write an opinion piece providing three reasons why they think their issue is important or problematic.

Grade and Standard	Typical Learners	Advanced Learners
Grade 5 W.5.1. Write opinion pieces on topics or texts, supporting a point of view with reasons and information.	Students will write a persuasive piece relating to a local issue that states their opinion, provides reasons, and includes a logical concluding statement.	After selecting a historical issue, advanced students will identify multiple perspectives about the issue and clearly state their opinion. They will provide reasons supporting their opinion and reasons for alternative views before framing a conclusion.
Grade 8 W.8.1. Write arguments to support claims with clear reasons and relevant evidence.	Students will write an opinion piece related to a local issue (e.g., building a local dump) in which opposing points of view are recognized, described, and rebutted.	After selecting a historical or global issue, advanced students will create opinion pieces, taking a definitive side of an issue. Each piece will identify multiple perspectives about the issue and clearly state the student's opinion. Students will provide reasons supporting their opinion and alternative views with support. Both primary and secondary sources should be used.
Grades 11–12 W.11–12.1. Write arguments to support claims in an analysis of substantive topics or texts, using valid reasoning and relevant and sufficient evidence.	Students will present arguments focused on a particular audience that has a different perspective than they do (e.g., extending the voting age to 21). They should formulate their argument to persuade and reflect the views and concepts of the opposing side.	After selecting a global issue of significance, advanced students will write two opinion pieces for two different audiences (e.g., paper on global warming to Democrats and to Republicans).

Subject: ELA Standards for Writing, *continued*

Strand and Number: Text Types and Purposes #2 (Informative, Explanatory)

Grade-Level Outcomes in Knowledge and Skills: Write informative/explanatory texts to examine and convey complex ideas and information clearly and accurately through the effective selection, organization, and analysis of content.

Note: This strand differentiation also contains differentiation of Standards 4–6: Production and Distribution of Writing and Standards and Standards 7–9: Research to Build and Present Knowledge.

Grade and Standard	Typical Learners	Advanced Learners
Grade 3 W.3.2. Write informative/explanatory texts to examine a topic and convey ideas and information clearly.	When provided a topic (e.g., Congress, solar system, famous people, current events), students will write an informational piece that includes details, facts, definitions, a conclusion, and a relevant illustration.	After selecting a topic of interest (e.g., Jupiter, history of the mandolin), advanced students will write a research piece providing definitions, facts, details (including appropriate graphics), and a conclusion that includes "so what/now what."
Grade 5 W.5.2. Write informative/explanatory texts to examine a topic and convey ideas and information clearly.	When given a menu of topics, students will select a topic of interest (e.g., Lexington and Concord, microscopic organisms). Their research should include facts, definitions, details, a concluding statement, and illustrations. Linking words and ideas should be present. Students should have a choice of media to share their products.	After selecting a topic of local significance (e.g., history of baseball), advanced students will write a research piece providing specific definitions, facts, and details (including appropriate graphics and organizational elements), and a conclusion that includes "so what/now what." Students will then translate the paper into a blog or a webinar.

Grade and Standard	Typical Learners	Advanced Learners
Grade 8 W.8.2. Write informative/explanatory texts to examine a topic and convey ideas, concepts, and information through the selection, organization, and analysis of relevant content.	When given a menu of topics (e.g., foreign customs, world events, life cycle of a forest), students will select a topic of interest. Their research should include facts, definitions, details organized by headings, a concluding statement, and illustrations. Linking words and ideas should be present. Students will then translate the paper into a PowerPoint or visual presentation.	After selecting an issue of local significance (e.g., global warming, investing in African economic development, comparing and contrasting their own community to Chicago from their reading activities), advanced students will write a research piece aimed at a particular audience for a particular purpose, providing specific definitions, vocabulary, facts, details (including appropriate graphics and organizational elements), and a conclusion that includes "so what/now what." Analogies and metaphors should be used to explain complexity and significance. Implications should be identified. Students will then translate the paper into a PowerPoint or visual presentation.
Grades 11–12 W.11–12.2. Write informative/explanatory texts to examine and convey complex ideas, concepts, and information clearly and accurately through the effective selection, organization, and analysis of content.	When given a menu of topics (e.g., foreign customs, world events, life cycle of a forest), students will select a topic of interest. Their research should include facts, definitions, domain-specific vocabulary, details organized by headings, a concluding statement, and illustrations. Details should include metaphors or similes to explain the complexity. Linking words and ideas should be present. Students will then translate the paper into a PowerPoint or visual presentation.	After selecting an issue of global significance, advanced students will write a research paper aimed at a particular audience for a stated purpose, providing appropriate organizational elements, a conclusion, and implications. Students will then translate and present the paper to an authentic audience through a self-selected visual presentation (e.g., film, webinar, blog).

Subject: ELA Standards for Writing, *continued*

Strand and Number: Text Types and Purposes #3 (Narrative)

Grade-Level Outcomes in Knowledge and Skills: Write narratives to develop real or imagined experiences or events using effective technique, well-chosen details, and well-structured event sequences.

Notes: This strand differentiation also contains differentiation of Standards 4–6: Production and Distribution of Writing. Although the standard appears to be similar across grade levels, there are developmental shifts within the process and products reflecting development of vocabulary, concepts, points of view, and interaction with literature. Advanced students' developmental trajectory of narrative writing should be faster pacing of skills and greater use of complex story lines and advanced vocabulary. The goals appear to be similar, but the outcomes are significantly advanced.

Grade and Standard	Typical Learners	Advanced Learners
Grade 3 W.3.3. Write narratives to develop real or imagined experiences or events using effective technique, descriptive details, and clear event sequences.	After reading Patricia MacLachlan's *Sarah, Plain and Tall*, students will write a story using dialogue, descriptions, narrator, sequence of events, and setting. Students will be presented a character from the book, a setting, and a sequence of events to place into a story line (e.g., a note that Sarah could write back home about meeting the family).	Advanced students will use the RAFT strategy (role, audience, format, and topic) to write a story, selecting from characters in Patricia MacLachlan's *Sarah, Plain and Tall*.

Grade and Standard	Typical Learners	Advanced Learners
Grade 5 W.5.3. Write narratives to develop real or imagined experiences or events using effective technique, descriptive details, and clear event sequences.	Given a piece of literature such as Frances Hodgson Burnett's *The Secret Garden*, students will write a story about a time they kept a secret.	Given a piece of literature such as Frances Hodgson Burnett's *The Secret Garden*, advanced students will retell the story from a different point of view and include specified literary elements.
Grade 8 W.8.3. Write narratives to develop real or imagined experiences or events using effective technique, relevant descriptive details, and well-structured event sequences.	Given a poem such as "Chicago" by Carl Sandburg, students will write a short story that takes place in Chicago.	Given a poem such as "Chicago" by Carl Sandburg, advanced students will write a historical fiction account, movie script, or play about an actual event in Chicago that impacted the city's development.
Grades 11–12 W.11–12.3. Write narratives to develop real or imagined experiences or events using effective technique, well-chosen details, and well-structured event sequences.	Given a historical or current event, students will write a narrative based upon the event.	Given a piece of narrative literature, advanced students will rewrite the story to capture experiences in a different way (e.g., rewrite "The Lottery" by Shirley Jackson without the experience of stoning).

Subject: ELA Standards for Writing, *continued*

Strand and Number: Production and Distribution of Writing #4–6

The majority of these standards are skills-based rather than being based on content or concepts, and as such, differentiation may be handled through the grade-specific types of writing in Standards 1–3. However, it should be noted that when the use of "peers" is denoted in the standards, appropriate advanced-level peers should be used to promote individual growth.

Strand and Number: Research to Build and Present Knowledge #7–9

Differentiation of these standards has been woven into the differentiation of the Informative/Explanatory writing standards and the Reading standards. It should be noted that although these standards do not start until grade 5, their use has been implemented in the differentiated Informative/Explanatory writing standards and the Reading standards by grade 3.

Strand and Number: Range of Writing #10

Differentiation of these standards has been woven into the differentiation of the Types of Writing standards and the Reading standards.

Subject: ELA Standards for Language

The examples provided to address the grammar standards use preassessment and streamlining as the differentiation techniques for accelerating basic content in both grammatical structures and usage. There is also the use of both complexity and creativity to provide open-ended opportunities in applying the principles of grammar and usage to selected text and to create one's own.

Strand and Number: Conventions of Standard English #1
Grade-Level Outcomes in Knowledge and Skills: Demonstrate command of the conventions of standard English grammar and usage when writing or speaking.

Grade and Standard	Typical Learners	Advanced Learners
Grade 3 L.3.1. Demonstrate command of the conventions of standard English grammar and usage when writing or speaking (including parts of speech, sentence structure, and verb tense).	Students are preassessed on prior learning in areas of the standard and are grouped according to results. Students are provided direct instruction in the terminology and application of grammatical forms and functions. Students create units of meaning using nouns, verbs, adjectives, and adverbs. Students then describe how the words are used in their units of meaning.	Advanced students are preassessed on prior learning in each area of the standard and are grouped according to results. Students receive streamlined instruction on the unlearned aspects of the standard by teaching form, function, and selective combination of words and usage principles through study guides and integrated task activities. Students create units of meaning based on the manipulation of cut-up words and describe the forms used (manipulate all parts of speech).

Grade and Standard	Typical Learners	Advanced Learners
Grade 5 L.5.1. Demonstrate command of the conventions of standard English grammar and usage when writing or speaking (including parts of speech, sentence structure, and verb tense).	Students are preassessed on prior learning in areas of the standard and grouped according to results. Students are provided direct instruction in the terminology and application of grammatical forms and functions. Students complete the following activity: • Step 1: Students read a passage from the text and indicate the parts of speech of underlined words. What purpose do these words serve in the sentence? Identify different sentence patterns that are used. How do they differ from each other? • Step 2: Students practice the application of parts of speech to their last writing paragraph. Tell how the words function in the piece. Identify key sentence structures that were used. How effective were they? • Step 3: Students use additional writing passages to practice analysis of grammatical structures (i.e., parts of speech and functions, sentence patterns). Students are posttested on key grammatical elements.	Advanced students are preassessed on prior learning in each area of the standard and grouped according to results. Students receive streamlined instruction on the unlearned aspects of the standard by teaching form, function, and selective combination of words and usage principles through study guides and integrated task activities. Students complete the following activity: • Step 1: Students read the text and identify (a) the parts of speech for underlined words, (b) the function in the sentence of underlined words, and (c) the sentence pattern used for each sentence in the passage. If the word is a verb, indicate tense. • Step 2: Students create a one-paragraph argument supporting the need for protection of endangered species. They provide three reasons to support their argument and conclude their paragraph. What are examples of each part of speech and its function in the paragraph? What sentence patterns were employed? • Step 3: Students respond to the following: How did the choice of grammatical structures help convey the message? In a group, share ideas and create a model for writing that could help students use varied sentence patterns, forms, and functions for words. Students are posttested when they are ready to show mastery of sub-elements of the standard.

Grade and Standard	Typical Learners	Advanced Learners
Grade 8 L.8.1. Demonstrate command of the conventions of standard English grammar and usage when writing or speaking (including use of verbals, tense, and voice).	Students will create a story using all forms of grammar (form, function, sentence patterns). In small groups, students will share the story and discuss verb forms used in respect to tense and voice.	Advanced students will analyze a short story, essay, or chapter for the use of all parts of speech, all functions, and three sentence patterns. They find or create the use of participles, gerunds, and infinitives and identify and justify the use of verb tense and voice. They answer the following questions for reflection: Why does grammar matter in communication? What is the special power of verbs?
Grades 11–12 L.11–12.1. Demonstrate command of the conventions of standard English grammar and usage when writing or speaking.	Students will apply standards of English usage and grammar in a persuasive essay in which they argue for free access to Internet materials.	Advanced students will apply standards of grammar and usage in multiple products (e.g., essay, multimedia project, debate) that support free access to the Internet. Students will analyze which approach to argumentation is the most successful for this issue and why.

Subject: ELA Standards for Language, *continued*

Strand and Number: Conventions of Standard English #2

Grade-Level Outcomes in Knowledge and Skills: Demonstrate command of the conventions of English capitalization, punctuation, and spelling when writing.

Grade	Typical Learners	Advanced Learners
Grades 3–8 Demonstrate command of the conventions of standard English capitalization, punctuation, and spelling when writing (including use of commas, quotation marks, possessives).	Students will provide a speech by a famous person and analyze why the use of punctuation is important, noting how it impacts meaning. (Look for use of commas, end punctuation, and other symbols.)	Advanced students will respond to the following task demands: • Step 1: Students will provide a speech by a famous person with all punctuation removed, and then will add it in and explain why it is appropriate. • Step 2: Students will analyze the same speech and change it by altering the use of commas and other punctuation to create a different emphasis or meaning within the text. • Step 3: Students will reflect on how punctuation affects meaning, tone, mood, and so forth.

Subject: ELA Standards for Language, *continued*

Strand and Number: Knowledge of Language #3

Grade-Level Outcomes in Knowledge and Skills: Apply knowledge of language to understand how language functions in different contexts, to make effective choices for meaning or style, and to comprehend more fully when reading or listening.

Grade	Typical Learners	Advanced Learners
Grades 9–12 Apply knowledge of language to understand how language functions in different contexts, to make effective choices for meaning or style, and to comprehend more fully when reading or listening.	Students will create a concept map for grammar and usage and describe what it represents in respect to language.	Advanced students will use a systems diagram to demonstrate how grammar and usage produce meaning in language. They will delineate elements, interactions, boundaries, and inputs that create such meaning and articulate their understanding of language as a system in a short essay.

Subject: ELA Standards for Speaking and Listening

The examples provided to address this standard focus on the differentiation features of complexity and creativity in respect to student presentations, based on research. Advanced students are expected to manipulate multimedia at higher levels of abstraction and demonstrate command of multiple variables in the process. Evaluative listening is also stressed, asking advanced students to make judgments about oral arguments.

Strand and Number: Comprehension and Collaboration #1

Grade-Level Outcomes in Knowledge and Skills: Prepare for and participate effectively in a range of conversations and collaborations with diverse partners, building on others' ideas and expressing their own clearly and persuasively.

Grade	Typical Learners	Advanced Learners
Grades 3–8 Engage effectively in a range of collaborative discussions (one-on-one, in groups, and teacher-led) with diverse partners on grade-level topics and texts, building on others' ideas and expressing their own clearly.	Students will participate in literature circles on grade-level topics.	Using Socratic seminars, advanced students will initiate and participate effectively in discussions on relevant real-world issues and key texts.
Grades 9–12 Initiate and participate effectively in a range of collaborative discussions (one-on-one, in groups, and teacher-led) with diverse partners on grades 9–10 (and 11–12) topics, texts, and issues, building on others' ideas and expressing their own clearly and persuasively.	Students will participate in face-to-face and virtual discussion groups on grade-level topics in language arts.	Advanced students will initiate virtual discussion groups on texts and topics of interest, posting and commenting regularly regarding text and ideas supported by textual evidence.

Subject: ELA Standards for Speaking and Listening, *continued*

Strand and Number: Presentation of Knowledge and Ideas #5

Grade-Level Outcomes in Knowledge and Skills: Make strategic use of digital media and visual displays of data to express information and enhance understanding of presentations.

Grade and Strand	Typical Learners	Advanced Learners
Grade 3 SL.3.5. Create engaging audio recordings of stories or poems that demonstrate fluid reading at an understandable pace; add visual displays when appropriate to emphasize or enhance certain facts or details.	Students will create audio recordings of a personally selected poem to demonstrate fluid reading and speaking skills.	Advanced students will create a podcast of a personally selected poem, varying voice and inflection to represent the speaker or tone of the poem.
Grade 5 SL.5.5. Include multimedia components (e.g., graphics, sound) and visual displays in presentations when appropriate to enhance the development of main ideas or themes.	After reading a book of their choice, students will create a video of themselves describing the plot and theme of the book to generate their classmates' interest in reading the book.	After reading a book of their choice, advanced students will create a video that captures the plot, theme, and characters of the book. The students will use the video as part of a presentation reviewing the text.
Grade 8 SL.8.5. Integrate multimedia and visual displays into presentations to clarify information, strengthen claims and evidence, and add interest.	Students are presented with textual information on a current event with the task of developing a presentation to teach their classmates about the topic.	Advanced students are presented with textual information on a current event with the task of developing a multimedia presentation with interactive elements to teach their classmates about the topic.
Grade 12 SL.11–12.5. Make strategic use of digital media (e.g., textual, graphical, audio, visual, and interactive elements) in presentations to enhance understandings of findings, reasoning, and evidence and to add interest.	At the conclusion of conducting research, students will develop multimedia presentations to present information to the classroom audience.	At the conclusion of conducting research, advanced students will develop interactive course sites (e.g., Blackboard or Moodle) that include audio, video, and interactive elements for the purpose of teaching others about the inferences and implications drawn from the research.

Using Cross-Disciplinary Content and Integrating Standards

Because standards often can be addressed across subject areas rather than only in one domain, we include examples of how to consider linking the CCSS for English Language Arts and the CCSS for Mathematics. We also suggest other areas of learning that can be applied to standards–based tasks to illustrate the efficiency and effectiveness that can be achieved through such compression and the differentiation for gifted learners that results.

There are two ways to remodel content to engage and motivate highly able learners by making cross–disciplinary connections. Although the strategies are related, they are distinct. The first approach is to use cross–disciplinary content. The second is to integrate standards from English language arts, mathematics, and other disciplines. Following are a few examples for each strategy.

Using Cross-Disciplinary Content

This strategy capitalizes on an area of interest in one discipline to engage learners in another. Begin with a standard from the CCSS for English Language Arts or Mathematics, and then draw in other content areas to give students opportunities to apply the standard. Examples are included below.

- *English Language Arts Standard W.5.7: Conduct short research projects that use several sources to build knowledge through investigation of different aspects of a topic.* This standard lends itself easily to a cross-disciplinary approach. Allow students to choose a topic that interests them on which to conduct the research. Then ask them to connect two areas of learning that relate to their area of interest. In an investigation of heroes in literature, for example, students might bring in art that illustrates the heroes studied and depicts their qualities. They might also link their study to real-world heroes today in the world of business and politics. What are the commonalities of literary and real-life heroes?

- *Mathematics Standard 3.OA.9: Identify arithmetic patterns (including patterns in the addition table or multiplication table), and explain them using properties of operations.* The idea in this standard is to identify and explain arithmetic patterns. Extend this idea beyond mathematics to motivate learners. What patterns might be identified for analysis in literature and language? Note that literature uses genres to illustrate patterns of meaning in different forms, and language provides patterns of form and function for units of meaning from words to sentences to paragraphs. Ask students to also identify and explain patterns in nature, in architecture, or in music.

- *Mathematics Standard 7.SP.4: Use measures of center and measures of variability for numerical data from random samples to draw informal comparative inferences about two populations.* Students can choose any content area to demonstrate mastery of this standard. For example, students could decide to determine whether the words in a chapter of a seventh-grade science book are generally longer than the words in a chapter of a fourth-grade science book.

Integrating Standards

This strategy combines standards from two or more disciplines to add complexity. Examples are included below.

- *English Language Arts Standard RF.5.3: Know and apply grade-level phonics and word analysis skills in decoding words. Use combined knowledge of all letter-sound correspondences, syllabication patterns, and morphology (e.g., roots and affixes) to read accurately unfamiliar multisyllabic words in context and out of context; and Mathematics Standard 5.OA.3: Generate two numerical patterns using two given rules. Identify apparent relationships between corresponding terms.* Ask students to list several syllabication patterns, and then generate numerical patterns that correspond to these same patterns.

- *English Language Arts Standard SL.K.5: Add drawings or other visual displays to descriptions as desired to provide additional detail; and Mathematics Standard K.G.5: Model shapes in the world by building shapes from components (e.g., sticks and clay balls) and drawing shapes.* Have students create a model of a city by using various shapes to represent different objects. Have them create a legend to demonstrate their use of shapes in the model. Finally, have them create a story about the city and illustrate it through photos, hand illustrations, or other visual displays.

Cross-disciplinary approaches are inherent in many research projects that students undertake. The writing demonstrates the capacity to build an argument, and the manipulation of data illustrates the capacity to interpret and transform ideas from graphic representations to verbal ones. By so doing, both English language arts and mathematics standards are addressed.

Differentiating Assessments to Encourage Higher Level Reasoning and Creativity

Although end-of-grade performance expectations are identified in the Common Core State Standards, teachers must also consider how differentiation of classroom assessments can be tailored to support the ongoing development of each student's literacy and numeracy in order to meet gifted students' unique academic and social-emotional needs.

In English language arts, curriculum may be modified with more advanced content (more difficult material, greater depth of exploration), more challenging readings (better aligned with students' reading levels), and projects that challenge students to stretch beyond their current level of performance through assessments that appropriately gauge the growth of the advanced learner. With the ELA standards' inclusion of literacy development across subject areas, ample opportunities for interdisciplinary and interest-driven learning are possible but require careful instructional design so that gifted students are afforded learning geared to their continued development as assessed regularly by the classroom teacher. Product-based assessment is a crucial approach in this process.

In reading literature and informational text, assessments should demand that students are able to transfer ideas and understandings about literary form and themes from text studied to text never before encountered. Performance-based assessments that require transfer of higher level thinking and problem solving, given a new textual stimulus, should be employed.

An example follows, based on a National Assessment of Educational Progress model from 1992 (NAGB, 2001):

Given a new text example, discern the main idea of the text.
- Explicate a few key lines from the text.
- How does the concept of _____ work in this text?
- If you were to change the title of the text, what might it be and why?

Dimensions of the task demand to be assessed would be:
- inference skills in discerning theme,
- analysis skills in explaining meaning,
- abstract thinking and concept development skills in discussing how a big idea permeates a work, and
- creativity and analytical skills in retitling and justification.

In addition, in order to provide qualitative feedback to the students, the prompt used could include a series of open-ended questions, such as: What were the strengths of the student work? What are the areas for improvement? The scale might be 1–4, with 4 representing an exemplary response, 3 representing a good response, 2 representing a limited response, and 1 representing a poor response. This assessment approach may be used with both literature and informational text, as it tracks well with the demands of both standards for the internalization of higher level thinking about what is read.

In writing, the assessment approach should be to use a prompt for the type and form of writing to be elicited. For example, a prompt for persuasive writing might ask students: Should cell phones be allowed in schools? In 30 minutes, they must craft a response that includes the following:

- an introduction that contains a claim,
- three reasons for the claim they have made,
- supporting ideas to substantiate each reason, and
- a conclusion that echoes the claim.

To provide qualitative feedback, the prompt could include open-ended questions, such as: What were the strengths of the student work? What are the areas for improvement? A 1–4 scale may be used to document a poor, limited, good, or exemplary response for each of the elements noted above. For a complete copy of a sample rubric, please refer to the Persuasive Writing Scoring Rubric in VanTassel-Baska and Little (2011). This rubric has been used in several studies in the language arts to show growth of both gifted and nongifted groups in persuasive writing (see Burkhalter, 1995; VanTassel-Baska, Avery, Little, & Hughes, 2000).

For the speaking and listening standard, a presentation rubric that penetrates the intention of the standard may be used. For example, a standard that calls for the use of multimedia to present a text and its ideas may use the rubric in Figure 1, modeled after several used in the William and Mary curriculum materials (available at http://education.wm.edu/centers/cfge/curriculum/languagearts/index.php).

The assessment approach for use with the grammar standard for advanced learners should consist of two types. One would be a pre-post assessment that focuses on students' ability to demonstrate mastery of parts of speech, how they function in sentences, and sentence patterns. A second would be a product assessment where students create text in a particular form that correctly uses all forms, functions, and selective combinations of words. They would also be asked to write a reflection statement on their developed piece as to how use of varied sentence patterns and forms create a more interesting piece of writing. A rubric that would assess the latter approach is shared in Figure 2.

Dimensions Assessed	Scale			
Clarity of presentation	4	3	2	1
Organization of material	4	3	2	1
Use of multimedia	4	3	2	1
Comprehensiveness	4	3	2	1
Creativity	4	3	2	1

Scale:
4 = Exemplary
3 = Good
2 = Limited
1 = Poor

1. What were the strengths of this project?

2. What were the greatest areas for improvement?

Figure 1. Sample presentation rubric for the speaking and listening standard.

Dimensions Assessed	Scale			
Accuracy of forms	4	3	2	1
Accuracy of functions	4	3	2	1
Sentence pattern accuracy	4	3	2	1
Reflection statement	4	3	2	1

Scale:
4 = Exemplary
3 = Good
2 = Limited
1 = Poor

1. What were the strengths of this project?

2. What were the greatest areas for improvement?

Figure 2. Sample rubric for the grammar standard.

Talent Trajectory: Creating Pathways to Excellence in English Language Arts

In preparing subject-area content for advanced learners, it is essential to look beyond grade-level cluster considerations to the bigger picture of their goals and aspirations for work in the adult world of the professions. Each advanced learner may bring an idiosyncratic vision to the task of mapping out a career development path. However, it is essential that we see the CCSS not as an end in learning itself but rather as a set of experiences that will advance students to the next level of interest, motivation, and capacity to perform in domain areas that will enrich their lives and ours. We have tried to think about the set of knowledge, skills, and experiences that gifted students use to develop excellence within a number of different fields. This set of experiences over time becomes the trajectory for high-level talent development in specific fields.

The conception of the trajectory is derived from the Gagné (2000) model of talent development that posits starting with abilities in different domains that become converted over time, learning, and practice routines into developed talents in various fields. The catalytic converter that affects this process is the dual roles of internal personality and motivational characteristics and external environmental factors like people in your life, nurturing experiences, and chance that affect the outcome for forging a creative, productive professional life. As we thought about this model, we were able to identify key interventions at different stages of development that would be important to consider in school-based curriculum and programming considerations for these students as they negotiate a talent development trajectory.

It may be important to lay out certain assumptions about our thinking in this regard:

- Talent development is a larger process than what happens during K–12 and is certainly bigger than what happens in school. Many of the experiences that matter for these students, based on the literature that informs our understanding of talented adults, occur outside of school and in more informal contexts that allow for the hours of practice necessary to convert skills to talents.

- The factors that influence the talent development process must merge in important ways: The individual must be willing to devote time and energy to a particular type of endeavor over multiple years and receive the instruction and support in that area that will fuel performance.

- The levels of talent that are reached may be affected by many variables, which include initial abilities, hours of deliberate practice, and the role of life occurrences that may inhibit as well as propel the person forward in the process. Thus, advanced learners may or may not fulfill their talent potential.

Optimal Match Fields for Advanced Language Arts Students

There are many high-level professions in English language arts that may provide an optimal match for the developed abilities of advanced learners in this subject area. Excellence may be attained in the pragmatic fields of law, translation, and politics; in the creative fields of writing poetry, novels, lyrics, or plays and in the world of acting; or in the synthetic fields of leadership in business, education, and government. Each of these fields requires the knowledge and skills of high-level oral and written communication manifested in multimedia, the trained intuition of timing and aptness of response, and the capacity to motivate and excite others on behalf of an idea.

The deliberate planning of interventions that may aid advanced learners in the journey toward excellence in a preferred area is a critical part of career preparation for them. It involves the synergy of building a plan across years that responds to their interests and needs at different stages of development and that acknowledges the importance of nurturing affective characteristics like risk-taking and relationships with others as well as the development of cognitive skills that provide a balance in their lives of work and play.

Stages of Development

Early years. Some of these interventions crucial at early stages of development include finding a peer group of students with similar interests and abilities who can work together. Grouping of gifted learners early is a spur to their developing abilities and interests in a verbal area. This is especially important for verbal learners, as research suggests that their growth and development is dependent on the verbal transaction process of trying out ideas as they are formulated (VanTassel-Baska, Zuo, Avery, & Little, 2002). Also critical at this early stage is providing rich experiences in all of the verbal arts stimulus areas, including reading, writing, viewing, drawing, and speaking. After a time, advanced learners may gravitate more to one area of the verbal arts than others by showing a clear preference for speaking, writing, or reading. Because we know that reading feeds the soul of writers, this preference may not signal a career path but merely an early preparatory predisposition.

Middle years. At the next level of development, advanced learners become more serious about their preferences and how they use time in pursuit of their talent. Gifted and advanced students may enter writing or forensic competitions to establish benchmarks that delineate their current progress and show how much advancement is needed to improve significantly at the process. Tutors or mentors who can provide assistance in the acquisition of skills at this stage of development can be valuable. In addition, it may be helpful to identify writers to emulate and serve as role models for spurring higher level development of a particular form. Other instruction and supports for growing interest at this stage include extracurricular camps and online programs in the summer or on Saturdays. Some students may begin to take world languages to hone skills and expand their vision and understanding of other cultures. This knowledge in turn aids in self-understanding and cultivates the empathy needed to develop meaningful relationships with others. Reflection on one's potential talent fields and a clear assessment of one's own strengths and weaknesses in the talent area provide another basis for judgment about how interested an advanced learner may remain in a worthwhile domain.

Adolescence. By adolescence, the development of talent is becoming more refined as advanced learners have opportunities to test out their skills in the adult world of work through apprenticeships and internships that provide glimpses of a future life that they may wish to experience. Their knowledge and skill bank is also growing through advanced in-school opportunities like Advanced Placement (AP) or International Baccalaureate (IB) English, History, or World Languages courses. Experiences at colleges and universities in coursework, in college and career planning, and in school-based advanced programs offer additional support during these years as the talent area emerges at a higher level, fueled also by performance and portfolio opportunities to showcase the actual work produced by the advanced learner at this stage. Competitions at the national and international levels become important to motivate the learner to higher levels of excellence in the selected area. Self-assessment becomes more integral to the advanced learner's decision making about col-

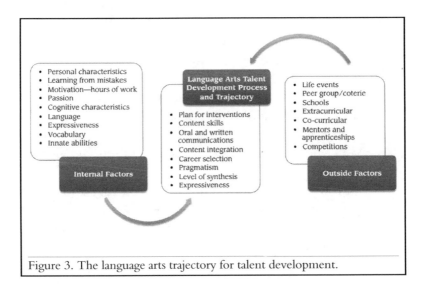

Figure 3. The language arts trajectory for talent development.

leges and programs of study that may be the optimal match for the evolving talent.

Figure 3 demonstrates the interplay of internal and external factors on the potential opportunities that advanced learners may experience as they move along the trajectory of talent development to a chosen profession aligned with their domain of strength and interest.

The Role of Schools in Talent Development

So what is the role of schools in this process? Can they become important brokers and facilitators of talent development, or do they become barriers to it by imposing cumbersome rules and regulations that block advanced learners from their upward trajectory of progress in a talent area? Hopefully, schools can begin to see how they can support the talent development process by becoming more flexible in how students are educated, when and where they are educated, and the levels of attainment that may be relevant given the students' advanced capacity and developed skills. For schools, the challenge is to step aside and find the optimal match for these students at a given point in time (Bloom, 1985). It is often not a desired role, as it requires humility in the face of a student who cannot be well-served by the existing system, creativity in finding the right resources that will help, and the follow-through to ensure that the intervention works for this advanced learner at a particular point in time. Counselors, teachers, and administrators all play important roles in this process of designing appropriate alternative intervention plans for advancing talent in specific learners, both individually and collectively.

Schools have an obligation not to make advanced learners "prisoners of time," and to ensure that their learning time is used efficiently and effectively as they traverse the grades (National Education Commission on Time and Learning, 1994). In suburban districts, that may mean being allowed to advance to the next level of coursework. In rural districts, it may mean having access to online coursework such as AP courses, which can be taken asynchronously. In specialized schools for the gifted, such as the New Orleans Center for Creative Arts, it may mean having an artist mentor working in a tutorial for portfolio development in lieu of classes one day a week. All of these options are appropriate for advanced learners, depending on the possibilities and constraints of the context.

Schools also have a special obligation to students from poverty to help them develop their talents. Unlike more affluent youngsters, these students lack the means of family support and resources that provide lessons, tutors, and extracurricular experiences through summer and academic year special programs (VanTassel-Baska, 2010). It is the schools themselves that must find creative ways to provide experiences to spawn the interest, the motivation, and the skill development necessary to make these students competitive in their desired future careers. A focus on a print-rich environment, vocabulary development, and discussion opportunities linked to writing all provide needed enrichment for such students. Special programs and services geared to these students must also be planned and executed so that talent is not denied based on means.

Implementing the Common Core State Standards With Various Program Models in Gifted Education

The models of delivery for advanced learners (or for any learner) are largely not addressed in the Common Core State Standards, allowing teachers and schools to implement services based on the needs of gifted students with the CCSS as a basis. Although gifted program design and delivery will be informed by these standards, programs and services for the gifted should be largely guided by assessment data about the abilities of students as well as best practices for serving them in each of the core subject areas.

As gifted program service models vary, so do the implementation implications for the CCSS. Gifted students receive services within heterogeneous settings, cluster-grouped classrooms, pull-out models, self-contained classrooms, special schools, and special classes.

Flexible Grouping in the Regular Classroom

For teachers of gifted and high-potential learners served in the heterogeneous, general education classroom with flexible grouping, the CCSS can serve as a benchmark for what all students should know, although educators should be careful not to limit curriculum for high-ability students based on the foundational expectations that would be provided to general education learners. In fact, those who are advanced may show mastery of content standards much sooner than other learners. As the CCSS authors acknowledge the limited nature of the standards in addressing the needs of the gifted, teachers must then modify learning experiences for these students (NGA & CCSSO, 2010a).

To address the curricular needs of gifted and high-potential students, teachers can differentiate curriculum through posing progressively more complex issues, adjustment of texts according to each student's reading level and interest, modification of mathematical processes according to those previously mastered, and pace of instruction. Although the CCSS provide indicators of general levels of performance for all students, teachers will need to modify learning so that gifted learners are provided appropriately challenging, stimulating experiences throughout the instructional day for continued progress.

Cluster Grouping

In cluster-grouped classrooms, teachers can use the CCSS as a basis for preassessment to determine where students are performing and adjust grouping according to students' abilities, interests, and strengths with respect to literacy. Teachers can group high-ability students flexibly throughout the school day to allow students the opportunity to regularly engage with peers of similar abilities and interests according to individual literacy skills addressed in the CCSS (e.g., speaking, reading, writing) or by a combination of skills.

Pull-Out Models

Teachers who serve gifted students in pull-out models, where gifted students spend a portion of their school day (or week) in a setting other than their general education classroom, are encouraged to consider how their infusion of literacy and numeracy address the CCSS and how the experiences in the pull-out setting offer advanced learning experiences beyond those that would be provided in the general education classroom. In addition to being informed of the content and scope of literacy experiences afforded to students in the general education classroom setting so that gifted program experiences may provide opportunities for greater depth, complexity, critical thinking, creative production, and research based on the individual needs of gifted students, teachers are also encouraged to use ongoing assessment information, including preassessments, to accommodate for the differences in ability between and among the students in the pull-out program.

Self-Contained

Gifted students who are served throughout the school day with gifted peers in self-contained classrooms engage in a range of literacy experiences as different content areas are addressed. Teachers of the gifted in these classrooms use the CCSS as a foundation for setting grade-level expectations, although gifted learners with advanced skills in literacy and numeracy often evidence proficiency early in the school year or acquire these foundational skills at a pace that is faster than their general education peers or even their gifted education peers. Thus, appropriate grouping within the self-contained classroom is recommended according to literacy and numeracy abilities. The curriculum should be qualitatively different from the curriculum offered to general education students according to the needs of individual students in terms of rate of learning, depth of content, difficulty of products, and complexity of thinking processes.

Special Schools

Special schools for gifted students are available for both elementary and secondary students. In general, the curriculum offered is both accelerated and enriched to provide accommodations for students who can handle work that is significantly more advanced than what is typical for their age–mates. Although these schools serve only students with gifts and talents and the curriculum offerings tend to be advanced, it is still vital that school personnel go beyond simply using the CCSS for a higher grade level when creating or aligning curriculum. Keeping in mind the natural progression of knowledge and skills, specialized schools must be certain that addressing any gaps in knowledge resulting from radical acceleration is a priority, particularly when students are pulled to the specialized school from many different educational settings. Despite the fact that the entire school is focused on students who spend their school day interacting with their intellectual peers, all of the gifted students in any particular class are not alike in their need for a different pace and differentiation in the complexity of the material being taught. The Common Core State Standards are an important tool to use in determining how to accommodate individual needs within a class.

Special Classes

Other than special schools, most of the programming options discussed above are used primarily at the elementary level, but there is no reason that these cannot be used at the secondary level, too. At the high school level, advanced learners are typically served through special classes that contain identified gifted learners and other learners at these levels. The emphasis of the coursework is on AP courses with more than 30 different subjects; the IB program, which is integrated across a prescribed course of study the last 2 years of high school; and dual enrollment, where high school students take a college-level course at a university or at their high school. Educators may believe that because upper level coursework is more specialized, those who take those courses are all advanced to the same degree. Simply because students are studying differential equations at the 10th-grade level does not mean that all students in the class are able to handle the same level of abstraction or can keep up with a fast pace. In a similar way, not all students in advanced language arts classes (honors) are at the same level with respect to analyzing literature, writing a persuasive argument, or completing a challenging research project. Great variation exists in the level of functional skills that students have acquired at any stage of development. Because language arts consist of multiple subjects, this is often the case with the sub-areas of learning. The CCSS can be used as a guideline to spur the necessary accommodations by looking across the standards for material to advance to the next level of learning. The standards may be calibrated to these advanced high school options; however, because the options are calibrated to college-level work, the standards inherent in the courses designed should take precedence.

Alignment of the Common Core State Standards With the Gifted Education Programming Standards

This booklet, designed around the Common Core State Standards for English Language Arts for use by teachers with gifted learners, was developed in alignment with both 21st century skills (Partnership for 21st Century Skills, n.d.) and the 2010 NAGC Pre-K–Grade 12 Gifted Programming Standards in key areas. The booklet is connected and integrated in important ways with multiple professional communities within gifted education and also across general education.

The NAGC Pre-K–Grade 12 Gifted Programming Standards represent the professional standards for programs in gifted education across P–12 levels. Within these standards, the curriculum and assessment standards were used to design the English language arts booklet in the following ways:

- *Development of scope and sequence*: This booklet has demonstrated a set of interrelated emphases/activities for use across K–12, with a common format and within key content strands.
- *Use of differentiation strategies*: The booklet developers used the central differentiation strategies emphasized in the

standards, including critical and creative thinking, problem solving, inquiry, research, and concept development.

- *Use of appropriate pacing/acceleration techniques, including pre-assessment, formative assessment, and pacing*: The booklet developers used all of these strategies as well as advanced literature to ensure an appropriate challenge level for gifted learners.
- *Adaptation or replacement of the core curriculum*: This booklet extends the Common Core State Standards by ensuring that gifted learners master them and then go beyond them in key ways. Some standards are mastered earlier (e.g., reading and language skills), and others are practiced at higher levels of skill and concept.
- *Use of culturally sensitive curriculum approaches leading to cultural competency*: This booklet's developers have employed world and multicultural literature to ensure that students have an appreciation for the contributions of different cultures to the literary canon.
- *Use of research-based materials*: The booklet developers have included models and techniques found to be highly effective with gifted learners in enhancing critical thinking, literary analysis, and persuasive writing. We have also used the questioning techniques found in Junior Great Books (Great Books Foundation, n.d.) and the William and Mary language arts curriculum (Center for Gifted Education, n.d.), both research-based language arts programs used nationally with gifted learners.
- *Use of information technologies*: The examples provided in this booklet suggest the use of visual media, computer technology, and multimedia in executing the learning activities developed.
- *Use of metacognitive strategies*: The booklet developers included activities for which students use reflection, planning, monitoring, and assessing skills.
- *Use of community resources*: This booklet includes opportunities for students to learn from a panel of experts or

to interview a relevant person central to understanding some aspect of a given unit of study.

- *Development of career pathways*: This booklet includes biography and autobiography as deliberate tools for students to model on an eminent person in the language arts such as a poet, novelist, or orator.
- *Talent development in areas of aptitude and interest in various domains (cognitive, affective, aesthetic)*: This booklet presents examples that provide multiple opportunities for students to explore domain-specific interests such as writing, viewing, and oral expression, exercising multiple levels of skills in cognitive, affective, and aesthetic areas.

Implications for Professional Learning When Implementing the Common Core State Standards

Professional learning is essential for all educators to increase effectiveness and results for students (Learning Forward, 2011). Teachers and content specialists should collaborate in learning communities to identify specific knowledge and skills needed to serve different groups of learners. As schools and school districts adopt and begin using the Common Core State Standards, all educators should be involved in ongoing learning to address the needs of gifted and high-potential students. Specifically, all educators need a repertoire of research-supported strategies to deliberately adapt and modify curriculum, instruction, and assessment within the framework of the CCSS, based on the needs of gifted students as well as those with high potential.

Although the CCSS provide the framework for the learning experiences for all students, gifted educators need focused training that is content-specific for differentiating the standards (VanTassel-Baska, 2008; VanTassel-Baska et al., 2008). Systematic professional learning will support all educators to adapt, modify, or replace the CCSS based on the needs of the learner. To differentiate effectively for gifted and high-potential learners, all educators need to develop expertise at designing learning experiences and assessments that are conceptually advanced, challenging, and complex.

Professional learning for implementing the CCSS for gifted and advanced learners should focus on evidence-based differentiation and instructional practices as they relate to specific core content. The training should demonstrate how and when to apply acceleration strategies; how to add depth and complexity elements such as critical thinking, creative thinking, problem solving, and inquiry; and how to develop and encourage innovation, all within the CCSS. In addition to the curriculum adaptation and modification, the professional learning experiences should also demonstrate content-specific ways to design and implement differentiated product-based assessments as well as pre- and postassessments appropriate for advanced students. However, gifted educators are in no way expected to be experts in all content areas; therefore, it is imperative to develop collaborative relations with skilled content specialists to provide knowledgeable advice, content-specific peer coaching services, and pedagogical knowledge while implementing the CCSS.

Examples of Professional Learning Models for Implementing the CCSS

Educators should take an active role in designing options to facilitate their learning and improvement of student results (Learning Forward, 2011). Active learning may include any of the following elements:

- discussion and dialogue,
- coaching and modeling,
- demonstration and reflection,
- inquiry and problem solving, and
- a tiered model of professional learning experiences (Learning Forward, 2011).

Discussion and dialogue. A professional learning community (PLC) of 3–6 teachers may agree to work together to improve their practice and student results (Lieberman & Miller, 2008). The PLC would identify specific learning standards for its grade and subject within the CCSS. During regularly scheduled meetings, the group of teachers would share ideas on ways to teach the standard, including ideas for differentiating learning experiences for advanced learners. The teachers of the PLC would identify strategies from the discussions, implement them in their classrooms, and then share their experiences when the group meets again. Ideally, the PLC would have collaboration and support from a gifted education specialist to provide ideas and resources for studying and practicing effective differentiation for gifted students.

Coaching and modeling. Learning options can include collaborative relationships such as mentoring or coaching. Specifically, peer coaching as a form of job-embedded professional development provides teachers a natural support system that can enhance teacher performance by the privileged sharing of knowledge and expertise through collaboration (Little, 2005). Whether it is the gifted educator serving as a peer coach or the one being coached, the coach may assume various roles, including content expert, classroom helper, teacher observer, and instructional facilitator (Cotabish & Robinson, 2012; Dailey, Cotabish, & Robinson, in press).

Demonstration and reflection. Demonstrations are a great way for teachers to learn new practices within authentic contexts. Professional learning leaders (Learning Forward, 2011) can work with teachers to demonstrate differentiation strategies within the CCSS. Examples of this model may include a teacher who is skillfully using preassessment to diagnose learner readiness and is providing differentiated tasks based on the results. The organizer of the professional learning would arrange for teacher learners to observe the demonstration one or more times and have them then practice the strategy in their classrooms. Ultimately the active demonstration strategy is enhanced by reflection on what was learned and how the implementation improved student engagement and performance.

Inquiry and problem solving. Inquiry and problem solving are techniques involving action research by a teacher or team of teachers. In the action research process, teachers examine their own educational practice systematically and carefully using techniques of research. The inquiry conducted by the teacher or team will generate data to inform or change teaching practices. One of the primary benefits of an action research approach to professional learning is the immediacy and proximity of the inquiry within the expected content of the curriculum. For instance, a teacher or a group of teachers may decide to study the effects of providing differentiated texts and instruction to advanced learners. Research techniques of measurement and consistent implementation would guide the inquiry with baseline assessment data for all students in the intervention as well as a control group if one is available. The teacher would implement the intervention (differentiated reading instruction) over a determined period of time and follow it with posttesting to look for changes in student achievement (within–subjects) or differences compared to the group without the intervention (between–subjects). Frequently, professional learning specialists help teachers develop ideas and data collection techniques for inquiry and problem solving.

A tiered model of professional learning experiences. In a tiered model of professional learning, the school or school district establishes clear expectations for developing expertise in gifted education and differentiated instruction (Johnsen, Kettler, & Lord, 2011). For gifted education professionals, the model would be built around the NAGC–CEC National Standards for Gifted Education Professional Development (Kitano, Montgomery, VanTassel-Baska, & Johnsen, 2008). Leaders within the school or school district would develop seminar learning experiences in which teachers would come together to learn differentiation strategies according to these tiered expectations (i.e., novice, intermediate, advanced). Experts in subject-specific differentiation would discuss and demonstrate specific ways to differentiate the CCSS across grade levels. These seminars would prepare teachers in specific content domains (e.g., mathematics) to practice evidence-based strategies for differentiating the CCSS for advanced learners. As teachers acquire expertise, they gradually move up the tiers from novice to intermediate to expert. As they reach expert levels, they begin to model the expertise and lead seminars with other teachers in their content area. The key ingredient is to provide clear guidelines of the skills expected to develop expertise in differentiating with the CCSS.

Collaboration With General and Special Education

It cannot be emphasized enough that gifted education professionals must collaborate with other educational partners and not "go it alone" in the process of implementing the CCSS on behalf of advanced learners and their talent development process. Gifted educators' responsibilities include direct service and advocacy for the gifted child, including academic, social, and emotional development. As a result of their training, gifted educators have extensive knowledge of strategy instruction, which allows for a deep understanding of pedagogy. However, it is important to recognize that giftedness impacts the whole child and that talent development involves both external factors and internal factors. There are numerous partners with whom it is important to collaborate, depending on the specific needs and abilities of the child.

- *Content experts.* When examining trajectories in English language arts and mathematics, it is critical that experts in these subject areas be involved in the process. Although gifted education specialists have significant training and expertise in strategy instruction, they must link to those people who have passion and expertise in the content areas so that students with promise and talent receive appropriate levels of instruction that are not tied to age or grade considerations.

- *Parents and families.* Although schools and educators play a critical role in the process of talent development, there is an equally important role of outside clubs, competitions, and community opportunities. Parents clearly play a role in mediating the selection and promotion of skills and activities in which students can engage. Parents must be perceived as both a source and a recipient of pertinent information, as well as a partner in the educational process.
- *Outside resources in the community.* Outside entities that promote specific content emphases must be approached as partners in the educational process. These entities can include online communities, colleges and universities, and different competition and contest organizations. Individuals affiliated with professional organizations might also provide connections to students and are valuable collaborators to facilitate talent development in a specific career pathway.
- *Special educators.* Understanding that gifted children may include students from diverse and special populations and may have multiple educational needs, gifted educators must collaborate with professionals who advocate and provide services for other special groups of students. Educators from special education (including ELL programs) and poverty-related programs play key roles in the development of talent in gifted children who are impacted by other factors within their lives.
- *Administrators.* Within their roles as gatekeepers and managers of the entire educational process, administrators must be included in discussions of systemic talent development. Rather than making talent development a highly individualistic, ad-hoc process, administrators can play a key role in systematizing an educational program that can provide progression within the disciplines for talented students.

A Possible Timeline for Implementing the Common Core State Standards Locally

Implementation of the Common Core State Standards at the K–12 level encompasses several varied but necessary tasks (see Table 1). For example, in English language arts, the standards must be examined for commonalities across standards such as in speaking and listening, which have properties in common with the writing and informational reading standards. A first step toward implementation is to become familiar with both the English language arts and the mathematics standards. Next, look at current practices, analyzing them to determine if there are gaps between current practices and practices that would reflect the CCSS. Where gaps have been identified, adjust content, process, products, and assessments to reflect the new English language arts and mathematics standards, bearing in mind that student outcomes should be aimed at developing expertise. Gather resources and consult with content specialists and gifted education specialists to assist with realignment. Consider the 2010 NAGC Pre-K–Grade 12 Gifted Programming Standards in the realignment process. Make sure the curriculum that is developed is coherent and focused on the development of concepts, not add-on activities. Provide professional development

Table 1

A Sample Timeline for Implementation of the CCSS

Task	Person(s) Responsible	When
Know and understand the CCSS for English Language Arts (ELA).	All school personnel	August–September
Gather evidence to determine the extent to which current practices reflect the practice standards; identify gaps in practice and/or content.	Teacher representatives at each grade level, building-level administrator, gifted specialist	October–December
Gather evidence to determine the extent to which current content reflects the content standards; identify gaps in practice and/or content.	Teacher representatives at each grade level, building-level administrator, gifted specialist, content specialist	October–December
Provide professional development to identify best practices in teaching ELA and adapting the CCSS for students with gifts and talents.	All teachers	January–March
Make adjustments to practices and content to reflect gaps that were identified, deleting curriculum that is not rigorous and does not meet the standards.	All teachers	January–March
Gather resources and assist with realignment to CCSS and to gifted education programming standards.	Gifted specialist, building-level administrator, content specialist, other necessary personnel	January–March
Provide professional development to prepare all teachers for full implementation of the CCSS for gifted and high-potential students.	Gifted specialist, building-level administrator, content specialist, other necessary personnel	April–July
Provide ongoing support for full implementation.	Gifted specialist, building-level administrator, content specialist, other necessary personnel	August–July

to ensure that school personnel understand the new standards and the changes needed to implement them for gifted and high-potential students.

Research Support for the Effort

The research support for the differentiation of the Common Core State Standards for English Language Arts to respond to the needs of the gifted is contained in several studies that have been conducted with both gifted and typical learners in classrooms across the country. Researchers suggest that using a differentiated curriculum and instructional plan designed for the gifted benefits both groups with respect to elevated learning in core language arts areas.

Feng, A. X., VanTassel–Baska, J., Quek, C., Bai, W., & O'Neill, B. (2005). A longitudinal assessment of gifted students' learning using the Integrated Curriculum Model (ICM): Impacts and perceptions of the William & Mary language arts and science curriculum. *Roeper Review, 27,* 78–83.
Abstract: The purpose of this study was to evaluate the effects of the William and Mary language arts and science curriculum, designed around the Integrated Curriculum Model (ICM), in a Northeastern suburban school district. The sample consisted of 973 students in grades 3–9. The effect size ranged from .52 to 1.38, and the overall academic growth increased in all of the

assessed domains. The results suggested that repeated usage of the William and Mary units yielded an increase in achievement in all tested areas of the language arts.

Kanevsky, L. (2011). Deferential differentiation: What types of differentiation do students want? *Gifted Child Quarterly, 55,* 279–299.

Abstract: Deferential differentiation occurs when the curriculum modification process defers to students' preferred ways of learning rather than relying on teachers' judgments. The preferences of 416 students in grades 3–8 identified as gifted for features of differentiated curriculum recommended for gifted students were compared with those of 230 students not identified as gifted. While thinking of their favorite school subject, participants responded to the 110 items on the Possibilities for Learning survey. Most and least popular items were reported in nine thematic categories (pace, collaborative learning, choice, curriculum content, evaluation, open–ended activities, expert knowledge, teacher/student relationship, and sharing learning). Self-pacing, choice of topic, and choice of workmates were most popular with students in both groups. Compared with nonidentified students, more of the students identified as gifted wanted to learn about complex, extracurricular topics and authentic, sophisticated knowledge and interconnections among ideas; to work with others some of the time; and to choose the format of the products of their learning. More students identified as gifted also disliked waiting for the rest of the class and asking for help. Overall, the groups' preferences differed in degree rather than kind and reflected cognitive abilities frequently cited as distinguishing characteristics of learners with high ability.

Mills, C. J., Stork, E. J., & Krug, D. (1992). Recognition and development of academic talent in educationally disadvantaged students. *Exceptionality, 3,* 165–180.

Abstract: Thirty-six students who scored average on standardized achievement tests and were economically disadvantaged were provided with a program to enhance their mathematics or language arts ability. Twenty-eight students served as a comparison group and received no treatment. After the intervention, the majority of students in the treatment group qualified for academically gifted programs.

Roe, M. F. (2010). The ways teachers do the things they do: Differentiation in middle level literacy classes. *Middle Grades Research Journal, 5,* 139–152.

Abstract: In this qualitative study, the author explored the concept of differentiation in urban, suburban, and rural language arts classrooms. The overall goal of understanding how differentiation occurred in these classrooms led to the following specific intentions: (a) to identify teachers' understandings of differentiation; (b) to understand their implementation of differentiated instruction for their students, especially those who underachieve or those for whom English is a second language, across an academic year; and (c) to understand students' and teachers' views of the challenges and successes of differentiation attempts. Using data collected from the classrooms of nine teachers and across 135 classroom observations and interviews with students and teachers, the author unveiled the following attributes linked to these teachers' differentiation practices: (a) differentiation is more than a classroom event, (b) the classroom climate contributes to differentiation options and practices, (c) differentiation entails attention to affective and cognitive variations, and (d) activities drive differentiation practices.

Swiatek, M. A., & Lupkowski-Shoplik, A. (2000). Gender differences in academic attitudes among gifted elementary school students. *Journal for the Education of the Gifted, 23,* 360–377.

Abstract: This study examined gender differences in attitudes toward academic subjects in 2,089 gifted students in grades 3–6. Observed gender differences were consistent with those found in research with older students. Grade-level differences suggest that attitudes toward several academic areas become more negative with age. Attitudes were not related to tested academic ability.

VanTassel-Baska, J., Avery, L. D., Little, C., & Hughes, C. (2000). An evaluation of the implementation of curriculum innovation: The impact of the William and Mary units on schools. *Journal for the Education of the Gifted, 23,* 244–272.

Abstract: Based on focus groups, interviews, documents, and classroom observations of schools implementing the William and Mary language arts and science curricula, it was found that students, teachers, parents, and administrators observed increased student engagement in class, enhanced reasoning skills, and the improvement of habits of mind, including metacognition.

VanTassel-Baska, J., Bracken, B., Feng, A., & Brown, E. (2009). A longitudinal study of enhancing critical thinking and reading comprehension in Title I classrooms. *Journal for the Education of the Gifted, 33,* 7–37.

Abstract: To measure gains in reading comprehension and critical thinking in Title I schools, the researchers conducted a longitudinal study of William and Mary language arts units over a 3-year period. Using six different school districts, 2,771 students in grades 3–5 participated in the study. The results indicated that both the treatment and control groups made statistically significant gains in critical thinking. Although the differences between the two groups were not overwhelming, the scores favored the treatment group.

VanTassel-Baska, J., Johnson, D. T., Hughes, C. E., & Boyce, L. N. (1996). A study of language arts curriculum effectiveness with gifted learners. *Journal for the Education of the Gifted, 19,* 461–480.

Abstract: This study examined the effects of a 40-hour language arts curriculum unit on elementary students in grades 4–6 in selected school districts. The experimental groups improved significantly in all three dimensions of the performance-based assessments: writing, grammar, and syntactic forms and functions. The authors conclude that more targeted curriculum intervention that is aligned with specific assessments needs to occur in classrooms for gifted students.

VanTassel–Baska, J., & Little, C. A. (Eds.). (2011). *Content-based curriculum for high-ability learners* (2nd ed.). Waco, TX: Prufrock Press.

Abstract: Research-based curriculum models based on effectiveness studies in science, social studies, and language arts are discussed based on the Integrated Curriculum Model and consequent effectiveness studies related to the model and curriculum for gifted students. Chapters with relevant examples for each core content area as well as an outline of the Integrated Curriculum Model are included.

VanTassel–Baska, J., & Stambaugh, T. (2006). Project Athena: A pathway to advanced literacy development for children of poverty. *Gifted Child Today, 29*(2), 58–63.

Abstract: This article reports the efficacy of using the *Jacob's Ladder* program with Title I students in order to elevate their reading comprehension skills to the level of critical reading and thinking. The program has shown significant growth for students at elementary levels and suggests that both higher level questions and activities promote such growth.

VanTassel–Baska, J., Zuo, L., Avery, L. D., & Little, C. A. (2002). A curriculum study of gifted-student learning in the language arts. *Gifted Child Quarterly, 46*, 30–44.

Abstract: Forty-six schools from 17 public school districts and one private school provided student data for this quasi-experimental study. Receiving language arts instruction in either a treatment or control group were 2,189 gifted students in grades 2–8. Students in treatment groups received instruction organized around the Integrated Curriculum Model from teachers trained in the curriculum materials. Overall, the results showed that the William and Mary units produced significant gains for gifted learners in higher order thinking and performance in core language arts areas.

Resources to Assist With the Implementation Process

There are a variety of resources that can assist university personnel, administrators, and coordinators of gifted programs at state and local levels in implementing the new CCSS for gifted learners, including assessments that measure the depth and breadth of a student's knowledge within a domain of talent development; curriculum units of study that are already differentiated and research-based; instructional strategies that employ the use of higher order thinking skills; and programming options that include appropriate pacing, rigor, innovation, and extended learning beyond the classroom.

The 2010 NAGC Pre-K–Grade 12 Gifted Programming Standards should be used as a tool to understand the elements that a differentiated curriculum for the gifted learner would include. For university personnel, it would be helpful to review the Teacher Preparation Standards in Gifted Education (NAGC & CEC, 2006) to see the extent to which there is alignment to the CCSS.

What follows is a sampling of resources that might be considered when implementing the CCSS with gifted students.

Assessment

Johnsen, S. K. (Ed.). (2012). *NAGC Pre-K–Grade 12 Gifted Education Programming Standards: A guide to planning and implementing high-quality services.* Waco, TX: Prufrock Press.

Sulak, T. N., & Johnsen, S. K. (2012). Assessments for measuring student outcomes. In S. K. Johnsen (Ed.), *NAGC Pre-K–Grade 12 Gifted Education Programming Standards: A guide to planning and implementing high-quality services* (pp. 283–306). Waco, TX: Prufrock Press.

Assessments for measuring the progress of gifted and talented students may be found in the *NAGC Pre-K–Grade 12 Gifted Education Programming Standards: A Guide to Planning and Implementing High-Quality Services* (Johnsen, 2012). Sulak and Johnsen (2012) described informal assessments that can be used informally in assessing student outcomes in creativity, critical thinking, curriculum, interests, learning and motivation, and social–emotional areas. They have also identified specific product and performance assessments and other assessments that might be useful in program planning and evaluation. Although many of the assessments do not have technical information, 23 do provide either reliability or validity information.

Partnership for Assessment of Readiness for College and Careers
    The Partnership for Assessment of Readiness for College and Careers (PARCC) is a 24-state consortium that has been formed to develop a common assessment system to measure the CCSS. To learn more about its work and the progress of its assessment development, visit http://www.parcconline.org/about-parcc.

Robins, J. H., & Jolly, J. L. (2011). Technical information regarding assessment. In S. K. Johnsen (Ed.), *Identifying gifted students: A practical guide* (2nd ed., pp. 75–188). Waco, TX: Prufrock Press.

Information regarding standardized achievement tests may be found in *Identifying Gifted Students: A Practical Guide* (Robins

& Jolly, 2011). In their chapter, Robins and Jolly provided a list of 28 instruments that are frequently used in the identification of gifted students and their technical qualities. Because many of these assessments are also used to identify students who are above grade level in specific academic areas, they would be appropriate for measuring a gifted student's academic progress.

Smarter Balanced Assessment Consortium

Smarter Balanced Assessment Consortium is a state-led consortium working to develop assessments that are aligned to the CCSS. The web-based resources include the alignment of the CCSS to International Baccalaureate, the Texas College Career Readiness Standards, depth of knowledge, and breadth of coverage within a domain. To learn more about the consortium, alignments with other standards, and the consortium's progress on developing assessments for the standards, visit http://www.smarterbalanced.org.

VanTassel-Baska, J. (Ed.). (2008). *Alternative assessments with gifted students*. Waco, TX: Prufrock Press.

The importance of appropriate assessment of gifted students in order to show growth is highlighted in this NAGC service publication. Separate chapters by noted authorities in gifted education focus on assessment issues related to both identification and learning. The book includes chapters on performance-based assessments, off-level assessment, products, and portfolios as more authentic ways to assess gifted student learning.

Curriculum and Instructional Strategies

Carnegie Mellon Institute for Talented Elementary and Secondary Students

The Carnegie Mellon Institute for Talented Elementary and Secondary Students (C-MITES) offers resources and links to curriculum in mathematics, science, technology, engineering, language arts, and social studies. For more information, visit http://www.cmu.edu/cmites.

Center for Gifted Education at The College of William and Mary

The Center for Gifted Education at The College of William and Mary has designed curricular units in the areas of mathematics, language arts, science, and social studies that are based on the three dimensions of the Integrated Curriculum Model: advanced content, higher level processes and products, and interdisciplinary concepts, issues, and themes. The materials emphasize a sophistication of ideas, opportunities for extensions, the use of higher order thinking skills, and opportunities for student exploration based on interest. Specific teaching strategies are also described on the website, including literature webs, the Hamburger Model for Persuasive Writing, a vocabulary web, the use of Paul's Elements of Reasoning, analyzing primary sources, and a research model for students. For more information about the units, visit the Center for Gifted Education at http://education.wm.edu/centers/cfge/curriculum/index.php.

Davidson Institute for Talent Development

The Davidson Institute for Talent Development offers links to resources in mathematics, language arts, science, social studies, arts and culture, and related domains. It also provides links to information about educational options such as ability grouping, acceleration, enrichment programs, competitions, and other services. To explore these resources, visit http://www.davidsongifted.org/db/browse_by_topic_resources.aspx.

Illinois State Board of Education

The Illinois State Board of Education provides Common Core State Standards resources for teachers and parents, including progressions in mathematics, lesson examples, and links to other resources. To access these resources, visit http://www.isbe.net/common_core/htmls/resources.htm.

Maine Department of Education

The Maine Department of Education provides resources for implementing the CCSS for language arts, including performance tasks and examples of student writing. For implementing the CCSS for mathematics, they have developed three modules that provide an overview, alignment with other standards, and professional development modules. To access these resources, visit http://www.maine.gov/education/lres/commoncore/index. html.

Neag Center for Gifted Education and Talent Development
    The Neag Center for Gifted Education and Talent Development offers online resources that describe research studies and defensible practices in the field of gifted and talented education. Some of the studies address curriculum at the high school level, the explicit teaching of thinking skills, cluster grouping, algebraic understanding, reading with young children, differentiated performance assessments, and content-based curriculum. To access the studies, visit http://www.gifted.uconn. edu/nrcgt/nrconlin.html.

Tools for the Common Core State Standards
    This blog from one of the authors of the Common Core State Standards provides news about tools that are being developed to support the standards' implementation. For more information, visit http://commoncoretools.me.

Gifted Education Programming

Colorado Department of Education
    The Colorado Department of Education provides *Gifted Education Guidelines and Resources* in programming for gifted and talented students that describe differentiated instruction for gifted learners (e.g., acceleration, content extension, higher order thinking skills), content options to address identified areas of strength, advanced learning plans, and acceleration tables. To retrieve the resources, visit http://www.cde.state.co.us/gt/ resources.htm.

Institute for Research and Policy on Acceleration

This website features *A Nation Deceived: How Schools Hold Back America's Brightest Students*, a two-part report that provides research-based information about acceleration and examines current practices. To download the entire report, visit http://www.accelerationinstitute.org/Nation_Deceived/Get_Report.aspx.

Purcell, J. H., & Eckert, R. E. (Eds.). (2006). *Designing services and programs for high-ability learners*. Thousand Oaks, CA: Corwin Press.

This book was designed as a workbook to develop effective programs and services for high-ability students. Each chapter provides a framework and guidelines for developing a key feature of gifted programming, from program mission statements and definitions of giftedness, to program design and curriculum.

Rogers, K. (2002). *Re-forming gifted education: How parents and teachers can match the program to the child*. Scottsdale, AZ: Great Potential Press.

Based on an analysis of a century's worth of research, Rogers presents information on specific aspects of gifted programming, including types of giftedness, gifts versus talents, assessment measures, parental guidance, acceleration, enrichment, group learning, independent study, education plans, working with schools, monitoring progress, and outside-of-school options. It includes tools to develop and maintain a plan to meet the learning needs of advanced students both in and outside of school.

References

Bloom, B. S. (Ed.). (1985). *Developing talent in young people*. New York, NY: Ballantine.

Burkhalter, N. (1995). A Vygotsky-based curriculum for teaching persuasive writing in the elementary grades. *Language Arts, 73,* 192–199.

Center for Gifted Education. (n.d.). *Language arts curriculum*. Retrieved from http://education.wm.edu/centers/cfge/curriculum/languagearts/index.php

Cotabish, A., & Robinson, A. (2012). The effects of peer coaching on the evaluation knowledge, skills of gifted program administrators. *Gifted Child Quarterly, 56,* 160–170. doi:10.1177/0016986212446861

Council of Chief State School Officers. (2011). *InTASC model core teaching standards: A resource for state dialogue*. Retrieved from http://www.ccsso.org/resources/programs/interstate_teacher_assessment_consortium_%28intasc%29.html

Dailey, D., Cotabish, A., & Robinson, A. (in press). Peer coaching in the elementary science classroom: A catalyst for success. *TEMPO*.

Gagné, F. (2000). Understanding the complex choreography of talent development through DMGT-based analysis. In K. A. Heller, F. J. Mönks, R. J. Sternberg, & R. Subotnik (Eds.), *International handbook for research on giftedness and talent* (2nd ed., pp. 67–79). Oxford, UK: Pergamon.

Great Books Foundation. (n.d.). *Junior great books.* Retrieved from http://www.greatbooks.org/programs-for-all-ages/junior/jgbseries

Johnsen, S., Kettler, T., & Lord, E. W. (2011, November). *Using the 2010 NAGC Pre-K–Grade 12 Gifted Programming Standards in professional development.* Paper presented at the annual meeting of the National Association for Gifted Children, New Orleans, LA.

Kitano, M., Montgomery, D., VanTassel-Baska, J., & Johnsen, S. (Eds.). (2008). *Using the national gifted education standards for PreK–12 professional development.* Thousand Oaks, CA: Corwin Press.

Learning Forward. (2011). *Standards for Professional Learning: Learning communities.* Retrieved from http://www.learning-forward.org/standards/learningcommunities/index.cfm

Lieberman, A., & Miller, L. (Eds.). (2008). *Teachers in professional communities.* New York, NY: Teachers College Press.

Little, P. F. B. (2005). Peer coaching as a support to collaborative teaching. *Mentoring and Tutoring, 13,* 83–94.

National Assessment Governing Board. (2001). *National Assessment of Educational Progress achievement levels 1992–1998 for reading.* Retrieved from http://www.nagb.org/publications/readingbook.pdf

National Assessment Governing Board. (2008). *Reading framework for the 2009 National Assessment of Educational Progress.* Retrieved from http://www.nagb.org/publications/frameworks/reading09.pdf

National Assessment Governing Board. (2010). *Writing framework for the 2011 National Assessment of Educational Progress.* Retrieved from http://www.nagb.org/publications/frameworks/writing-2011.pdf

National Association for Gifted Children. (2010). *NAGC Pre-K–Grade 12 Gifted Programming Standards*. Retrieved from http://www.nagc.org/ProgrammingStandards.aspx

National Association for Gifted Children, & Council for Exceptional Children. (2006). *NAGC-CEC teacher knowledge and skills for gifted and talented education*. Retrieved from http://www.nagc.org/NCATEStandards.aspx

National Education Commission on Time and Learning. (1994). *Prisoners of time*. Retrieved from http://www2.ed.gov/pubs/PrisonersOfTime/index.html

National Governors Association Center for Best Practices, & Council of Chief State School Officers. (2010a). *Common Core State Standards for English Language Arts*. Retrieved from http://www.corestandards.org/the-standards

National Governors Association Center for Best Practices, & Council of Chief State School Officers. (2010b). *Common Core State Standards for English Language Arts and literacy in history/social studies, science, and technical subjects: Appendix B: Text exemplars and sample performance tasks*. Retrieved from http://www.corestandards.org/assets/Appendix_B.pdf

Partnership for 21st Century Skills. (n.d.). *Framework for 21st century learning*. Retrieved from http://www.p21.org/overview

VanTassel-Baska, J. (2008). An effective, standards-based professional development model for gifted education. In M. Kitano, D. Montgomery, J. VanTassel-Baska, & S. Johnsen (Eds.), *Using the national gifted education standards for preK–12 professional development* (pp. 49–54). Thousand Oaks, CA: Corwin Press.

VanTassel-Baska, J. (Ed.). (2010). *Patterns and profiles of promising learners from poverty*. Waco, TX: Prufrock Press.

VanTassel-Baska, J., Avery, L. D., Little, C., & Hughes, C. (2000). An evaluation of the implementation of curriculum innovation: The impact of the William & Mary units on schools. *Journal for the Education of the Gifted, 23*, 244–272.

VanTassel-Baska, J., Feng, A., Brown, E., Bracken, B., Stambaugh, T., & French, H. (2008). A study of differentiated instructional change over three years. *Gifted Child Quarterly, 52,* 297–312.

VanTassel-Baska, J., & Little, C. A. (Eds.). (2011). *Content-based curriculum for high-ability learners* (2nd ed.). Waco, TX: Prufrock Press.

VanTassel-Baska, J., Zuo, L., Avery, L., & Little, C. A. (2002). A curriculum study of gifted-student learning in the language arts. *Gifted Child Quarterly, 46,* 30–43.

Appendix A
Definitions of Key Terms

Acceleration is a broad term used to describe ways in which gifted student learning may occur at a fast and appropriate rate throughout the years of schooling. It refers to content acceleration through preassessment, compacting, and reorganizing curriculum by unit or year; grade skipping; telescoping 2 years into one; dual enrollment in high school and college or university; and more personalized approaches such as tutorials, mentorships, and independent research that would also be sensitive to the advanced starting level of these learners for instruction. Both Advanced Placement (AP) and International Baccalaureate (IB) at the high school level represent programs of study already accelerated in content. AP courses also may be taken on a fast-track schedule earlier as appropriate.

Appropriate pacing refers to the rate at which material is taught to advanced learners. Because they are often capable of mastering new material more rapidly than typical learners, appropriate pacing would involve careful preassessment to determine readiness for more advanced material to ensure that advanced learners are not bored with the material and are being adequately challenged. Note that although students might advance quickly through some material, they should also be given time to delve more deeply into topics of interest at appropriate advanced levels of complexity and innovation.

Assessment is the way to determine the scope and degree of learning that has been mastered by the student. For purposes of gifted education, the assessments must be matched to differentiated outcomes, requiring the use of authentic approaches like performance- and portfolio-based assessment demands. Some assessments are already constructed and available for use, exhibiting strong technical adequacy and employed in research studies, whereas others may be teacher-developed, with opportunities to establish interrater reliability among teachers who may be using the assessments in schools. Care should be taken to use assessments that do not restrict the level of proficiency that students can demonstrate, such as above-grade-level assessments, and that allow for innovative and more complex responses.

Characteristics and needs of gifted learners are the basis for differentiating any curriculum area. In English language arts, verbally talented students learn to read, talk in complex sentences, write coherent text, and become sensitive to language at an earlier stage of development than typical learners. Because of this advanced readiness to engage with their world, their curriculum may be accelerated and should be advanced, rich in experiences for increasing complexity and depth, and open-ended to allow for creative manipulation of ideas and concepts.

Complexity refers to a feature of differentiation that provides advanced learners more variables to study, asks them to use multiple resources to solve a problem, or requires them to use multiple higher order thinking skills simultaneously. The degree of complexity may depend on the developmental level of the learner, the nature of the learning task, and the readiness to take on the level of challenge required.

Creativity and innovation are used to suggest that activities conducted with the gifted employ opportunities for more open-ended project work that mirrors real-world professional work in solving problems in the disciplines. The terms also suggest that advanced learners are proficient in the skills and habits of mind associated with being a creator or innovator in a chosen field of endeavor. Thus, creative thinking and problem-solving skills would be emphasized.

Curriculum is a set of planned learning experiences, delineated from a framework of expectations at the goal or outcome level, that represent important knowledge, skills, and concepts to be learned. Differentiated curriculum units of study may have already been designed and tested for effectiveness in language arts, or units may be developed by teachers to use in gifted instruction.

Differentiation of curriculum for gifted learners is the process of adapting and modifying curriculum structures to address these learners' characteristics and needs more optimally. Curriculum goals, outcomes, and activities may be tailored for gifted learners to accommodate their needs. Typically, this process involves the use of the strategies of acceleration, complexity, depth, and creativity in combination.

Instruction is the delivery system for teaching that comprises the deliberate use of models, strategies, and supportive management techniques. For gifted learners, inquiry strategies such as Problem-Based Learning (PBL), Creative Problem Solving (CPS) and problem posing, and critical thinking models such as Paul's Reasoning Model used in independent research or within a flexible grouping approach in the regular classroom constitute instructional differentiation.

Rigor and relevance suggest that the curriculum experiences planned for advanced learners be sufficiently challenging yet provided in real-world or curricular contexts that matter to learners at their particular stage of development.

Streamlining is a process to shorten the amount of time that advanced students spend on basic material, even after their functional level is ascertained. Compressing the content into larger chunks of learning becomes the task for teachers in order to accommodate advanced student learning pace and rate.

Talent trajectory is used to describe the school span development of advanced learners in their area of greatest aptitude from

K–16. It is linked to developmental stages from early childhood through adolescence and defines key interventions that aid in the talent development process, specific to the subject area and desired career path.

Teacher quality refers to the movement at all levels of education to improve the knowledge base and skills of classroom teachers at P–12 levels, which is necessary for effective instruction for advanced students. It is the basis for a redesign of teacher education standards and a rationale for examining P–12 student outcomes in judging the efficacy of higher education programs for teachers. Policy makers are committed to this issue in improving our P–16 education programs.

Appendix B
Evidence-Based Practices
in Gifted Education

Evidence-based practices that inform the Teacher Preparation and Programming Standards in Gifted Education relate to assessment, curriculum, instruction, and grouping issues, all of which are embedded within the Common Core State Standards. These practices have an extensive research base. (The full references for the following citations can be found in the research base that accompanies the NAGC–CEC Teacher Preparation Standards in Gifted Education, available online at http://www.nagc.org.)

Assessment of Individual Characteristics and Needs
- Because of their advanced cognitive functioning, internal locus of control, motivation, and talents, teachers need to provide intellectual challenge in their classrooms to gifted and talented students (Ablard & Tissot, 1998; Barnett & Durden, 1993; Carter, 1985; Gross, 2000; McLauglin & Saccuzzo, 1997; Robinson & Clinkenbeard, 1998; Swiatek, 1993).
- Educators must also be receptive to gifted students' affective needs and sensitive to the socioemotional and coping needs of special groups of learners (e.g., highly

gifted, gifted students with disabilities, gifted students from diverse backgrounds, gifted girls, gifted boys; Albert & Runco, 1989; Coleman, 2001; Cross, Stewart, & Coleman, 2003; Ford & Harris, 2000; Gross, 2003; Kennedy, 1995; Peterson, 2003; Shaunessy & Self, 1998; Swiatek & Dorr, 1998).

- Gifted students' cultural, linguistic, and intellectual differences should be considered when planning instruction and differentiating curriculum (Boothe & Stanley, 2004).
- Educators need to use preassessment and ongoing assessment to adjust instruction that is consistent with the individual student's progress (Reis, Burns, & Renzulli, 1992; Winebrenner, 2003).
- Assessments used to document academic growth include authentic tasks, portfolios, and rubrics and performance-based assessments (Sheffield, 2003; Siegle, 2002; Treffinger, 1994; VanTassel-Baska, 2002).
- The results of progress assessments can be used to adjust instruction, including placement in appropriate group learning settings and academic acceleration (Feldhusen, 1996; Kulik, 1992).

Instruction
- Teachers need to use metacognitive and higher level thinking strategies in the content areas, activities that address the gifted students' areas of interest and foster research skills (Anderson & Krathwohl, 2001; Center for Gifted Education, 2000; Elder & Paul, 2003; Hébert, 1993; Johnsen & Goree, 2005; Moon, Feldhusen, & Dillon, 1994; VanTassel-Baska, Avery, Little, & Hughes, 2000).
- Educators should develop gifted students' use of cognitive strategies and encourage deliberate training in specific talent areas (Bloom & Sosniak, 1981; Ericcson & Charness, 1994; Feldman, 2003).

- Technology can be used in independent studies to access mentors and electronic resources and to enroll in advanced classes (Cross, 2004; Ravaglia, Suppes, Stillinger, & Alper, 1995; Siegle, 2004).

Curriculum

- In the classroom, curricular modifications for gifted students include acceleration, enrichment, grouping, Problem-Based Learning, curriculum compacting, tiered lessons, independent study, and specific curriculum models (Betts & Neihart, 1986; Brody, 2004; Colangelo, Assouline, & Gross, 2004; Gallagher & Stepien, 1996; Gavin, Casa, Adelson, Carroll, & Sheffield, 2009; Gavin & Sheffield, 2010; Gentry, 1999; Johnsen & Goree, 2005; Kulik & Kulik, 1992; Milgram, Hong, Shavit, & Peled, 1997; Renzulli & Reis, 2004; Rogers, 2003; Southern & Jones, 1991; Tomlinson, 2002; Tomlinson, Kaplan, Renzulli, Burns, Leppien, & Purcell, 2001; VanTassel-Baska & Little, 2003).
- Models emphasize the need for considering students' interests, environmental and natural catalysts, curriculum differentiation, and the development of higher level thinking skills (Elder & Paul, 2003; Gagné, 1995; Renzulli & Reis, 2003; Tomlinson & Cunningham-Eidson, 2003).
- When designing a differentiated curriculum, it is essential to develop a scope and sequence and align national, state or provincial, and/or local curricular standards with the differentiated curriculum (Maker, 2004; VanTassel-Baska & Johnsen, 2007; VanTassel-Baska & Stambaugh, 2006; Tassell, Stobaugh, Fleming, & Harper, 2010).
- Specific curricula have been designed for gifted students and include affective education, leadership, domain-specific studies, and the arts (Clark & Zimmerman, 1997; Nugent, 2005; Parker & Begnaud, 2003; VanTassel-Baska, 2003a).

- Educators should integrate academic and career guidance into learning plans for gifted students, particularly those from diverse backgrounds (Cline & Schwartz, 2000; Ford & Harris, 1997).
- Differentiated curricula results in increased student engagement, enhanced reasoning skills, and improved habits of mind (VanTassel-Baska, Avery, Little, & Hughes, 2000).
- When individuals from diverse backgrounds are provided challenging curricula, their abilities and potential are more likely to be recognized (Ford, 1996; Ford & Harris, 1997; Mills, Stork, & Krug, 1992).

Environment
- Working in groups with other gifted students and mentors can yield academic benefits and enhance self-confidence and communication skills (Brody, 1999; Davalos & Haensly, 1997; Grybe, 1997; Pleiss & Feldhusen, 1995; Torrance, 1984).
- Working under a successful mentor in an area of interest can foster personal growth, leadership skills, and high levels of learning (Betts, 2004; Brody, 1999; Davalos & Haensly, 1997; Feldhusen & Kennedy, 1988; Grybe, 1997; Pleiss & Feldhusen, 1995; Torrance, 1984).
- Other learning situations that support self-efficacy, creativity, and life-long learning include early college entrance programs, talent searches, math clubs and circles, online and afterschool/summer programs, competitions, Problem-Based Learning, independent play, independent study, and the International Baccalaureate program (Betts, 2004; Boothe, Sethna, Stanley, & Colgate, 1999; Christophersen & Mortweet, 2003; Gallagher, 1997; Johnsen & Goree, 2005; Karp, 2010; Olszewski-Kubilius, 1998; Poelzer & Feldhusen, 1997; Riley & Karnes, 1998; Rotigel & Lupkowski-Shoplik,

1999; Ruszcyk, 2012; Warshauer, McCabe, Sorto, Strickland, Warshauer, & White, 2010).

- Three factors need to be present for students to develop their talents: (a) above-average ability and motivation; (b) school, community, and/or family support; and (c) acceptance by peers in the domain of talent (Bloom, 1985; Csikszentmihalyi, 1996; Gagné, 2003; Renzulli, 1994; Siegle & McCoach, 2005).

About the Editor

Joyce VanTassel-Baska, Ed.D., is the Smith Professor Emerita at The College of William and Mary, where she developed a graduate program and a research and development center in gifted education. Formerly, she initiated and directed the Center for Talent Development at Northwestern University. She has also served as the state director of gifted programs for Illinois, as a regional director of a gifted service center in the Chicago area, as coordinator of gifted programs for the Toledo, OH, public school system, and as a teacher of gifted high school students in English and Latin. Dr. VanTassel-Baska has published widely, including 27 books and more than 500 refereed journal articles, book chapters, and scholarly reports. Her major research interests are the talent development process and effective curricular interventions with the gifted.

About the Contributors

Claire E. Hughes, Ph.D., is an associate professor at the College of Coastal Georgia in an integrated elementary/special education teacher preparation program. Dr. Hughes was recently a Visiting Fellow at Oxford. The author of two books on high functioning autism, her research areas include twice-exceptional children, cognitive interventions, and Response to Intervention.

Susan K. Johnsen, Ph.D., is professor in the Department of Educational Psychology at Baylor University, where she directs the Ph.D. program and programs related to gifted and talented education. She is the author of more than 200 publications, including *Identifying Gifted Students: A Practical Guide*, books related to implementing the national teacher preparation standards in gifted education, and tests used in identifying gifted students, and is the editor-in-chief of *Gifted Child Today*. She serves on the Board of Examiners of the National Council for Accreditation of Teacher Education, is a reviewer and auditor of programs in gifted education, and is chair of the Knowledge and Skills Subcommittee of the Council for Exceptional Children. She is past president of The Association for the Gifted (TAG) and past president of the Texas Association for the Gifted and Talented (TAGT).

Jennifer L. Jolly, Ph.D., is an associate professor at Louisiana State University in elementary and gifted education. Her research interests include the history of the field and parents of gifted children. She is also the editor-in-chief of *Parenting for High Potential.*

Todd Kettler, Ph.D., is an assistant professor in the Department of Educational Psychology at the University of North Texas. He has been a teacher of gifted students and a gifted program director. In his current role, he teaches graduate courses in gifted education.

Debra A. Troxclair, Ph.D., is an assistant professor in the Counseling & Special Populations Department at Lamar University, where she is the coordinator of the undergraduate special education program. She has more than 25 years of experience teaching at the elementary and middle school levels, and she has prepared teachers at the graduate and undergraduate levels in Louisiana, Mississippi, Alabama, and Texas.